Act Like a Lady, Think Like a Man

STEVE HARVEY

-WITH-

Denene Millner

Act Like a Lady,

—◆—

Think Like a

MAN

WHAT MEN REALLY THINK ABOUT LOVE,

RELATIONSHIPS, INTIMACY, AND COMMITMENT

Amistad

An Imprint of HarperCollins*Publishers*

This book is dedicated to all women.
My hope is to empower you with a wide-open
look into the minds of men.

HarperCollins books may be purchased for educational, business, or sales promotional use. For information please write: Special Markets Department, HarperCollins Publishers, 10 East 53rd Street, New York, NY 10022.

A hardcover edition of this book was published in 2009 by Amistad, an imprint of HarperCollins Publishers.

FIRST AMISTAD PAPERBACK EDITION PUBLISHED 2011.

Designed by Janet M. Evans

Library of Congress Cataloging-in-Publication Data has been applied for.

ISBN 978-0-06-172898-3

11 12 13 14 15   OV/RRD   10 9 8 7 6 5 4 3 2 1

CONTENTS

EVERYTHING YOU NEED TO KNOW ABOUT MEN AND RELATIONSHIPS IS RIGHT HERE

I've made a living for more than twenty years making people laugh—about themselves, about each other, about family, and friends, and, most certainly, about love, sex, and relationships. My humor is always rooted in truth and full of wisdom—the kind that comes from living, watching, learning, and knowing. I'm told my jokes strike chords with people because they can relate to them, especially the ones that explore the dynamics of relationships between men and women. It never ceases to amaze me how much people talk about relationships, think about them, read about them, ask about them—even get in them without a clue how to move them forward. For sure, if there's anything I've discovered during my journey here on God's earth, it's this: (a) too many women are clueless about men, (b) men get away with a whole lot of stuff in relationships because women have never understood how men think, and (c) I've got some valuable information to change all of that.

I discovered this when my career transitioned to radio with the *Steve Harvey Morning Show*. Back when my show was based in Los Angeles, I created a segment called "Ask Steve," during which women could call in and ask anything they wanted to about relationships. Anything. At the very least, I thought "Ask Steve" would lead to some good comedy, and at first, that's pretty much what it was all about for me—getting to the jokes. But it didn't take me long to realize that what my listeners, mostly women, were going through wasn't really a laughing matter. They had dozens of categories of needs and concerns in their lives that they were trying to get a handle on—dating, commitment, security, family baggage, hopes for tomorrow, spirituality, in-law drama, body image, aging, friendships, children, work/home balance, education. You name the topic, somebody asked me about it. And heading up the list of topics women wanted to talk about was—you guessed it—men.

My female listeners really wanted answers—answers to how to get out of a relationship what they're putting into it. On those "Ask Steve" segments, and later, through the "Strawberry Letters" segment I do on the current incarnation of the *Steve Harvey Morning Show*, women have made clear that they want an even exchange with men: they want their love to be reciprocated in the same way they give it; they want their romantic lives to be as rewarding as they make them for their potential mates; they want the emotions that they turn on full blast to be met with the same intensity; and they expect the premium that they put on commitment to be equally adhered to, valued, and respected. The problem for all too many women who call in to my radio show, though, is that they just can't get that reciprocation from men, and women then end up feeling disappointed, disenfranchised, and disillusioned by their failed relationships.

When I step back from the jokes, and the microphone gets turned off and the lights in the studio go down, and I think about what women ask me every morning on my show, I get incredibly perplexed—perplexed because even though my callers have all presumably had some experience with men (whether they are friends, boyfriends, lovers, husband, fathers, brothers, or co-workers), these women still genuinely want to know how to get the love they want, need, and deserve. I've concluded that the truths they seek are never as obvious to them as they are to us men. Try as they might, women just don't get us.

With this in mind, I stopped joking around and got very real with my audience. Through my answers, I started imparting wisdom about men—wisdom gathered from working more than half a century on one concept: how to be a man. I also spent countless hours talking to my friends, all of whom are men. They are athletes, movie and television stars, insurance brokers and bankers, guys who drive trucks, guys who coach basketball teams, ministers and deacons, Boy Scout leaders, store manager, ex-cons, inmates, and yes, even hustlers. And one simple thing is true about each of us: we are very simple people and all basically think in a similar way.

When I filter my answers through that lens of how men view relationships, the women in my audience start to understand why the complexities and nuances they drag into each of their relationships with the opposite sex really serve them no justice. I teach them very quickly that expecting a man to respond to them the way a woman would is never going to work. They then realize that a clear-eyed, knowing approach to dealing with men on their terms, on their turf, in their way, can, in turn, get women exactly what they want.

Indeed, my advice for the folks who called in on the "Ask Steve" segment of the *Steve Harvey Morning Show* became so popular that fans—women and men—started asking me when I was going to write a relationship book—something to help the women who genuinely want to be in a solid, committed relationship figure out how to get one, and help the men ready for those relationships to be recognized for what they can and are willing to bring to the table. I have to admit: I didn't really see the value of writing a relationship book at first. What, after all, did I have to add to the conversation beyond the answers I give to an audience of millions every morning? Even bigger than that, how could I be taken seriously? Hell, I'm not a writer.

But then I started thinking about the relationships that I've had in my lifetime, talked to some of my male friends and some of my female co-workers and associates, and put together a few informal focus groups. I considered the impact that relationships have on each of us, and especially the impact they've had on me. My father? He was married to my mother for sixty-four years. My mother was invaluable to him. And she was invaluable to me—the most influential person in my life. Equally valuable to me are my wife and my children. In fact, my girls and my concern for their future inspire me here as well. They will all grow up and reach for the same dream most women do: The husband. Some kids. A house. A happy life. True love. And I want desperately for my children to avoid being misguided and misled by the games men have created just to perpetrate the greed and selfishness we tend to show the world until we become the men God wants us to be. I know—because of my mother, my wife, my daughters, and the millions of women who listen to my show every morning—that women need a voice, someone to help get them through and decipher the muck, so they can get what they're truly after. I figured I could be that guy to wave across the fence and say, "I'm going to tell you the secrets—the real deal about men, the things we wish you knew about us, but that we really don't want you to know, lest we lose the game."

In essence, *Act Like a Lady, Think Like a Man* is a playbook of sorts. You remember how a few years back, the New England Patriots got accused of one of the biggest cheating scandals in NFL history? NFL investigators found out that the team had been secretly videotaping practices and reading mouths to figure out the plays of their opposing teams—a practice that gave them a distinct advantage over their rivals. For sure, the Patriots' dirty ways were almost as advantageous to the New England team as if they were reading the opposition's playbook. With the advantage, the Patriots were able to win games.

This is what I wish for the women who read *Act Like a Lady, Think Like a Man*. I want every woman who truly wants a solid relationship but just can't figure out how to get one, and those who are already in a relationship and trying to figure out how to make it better, to forget everything she's ever been taught about men—erase the myths, the heresy, everything your mother told you, everything your girlfriends told you, all the advice you've read in magazines and seen on television—and find out here, in these pages, who men really are. What men count on is that you'll continue to get your advice from other women who do not know our tactics or our mind-set. *Act Like a Lady, Think Like a Man* is going to change this for you. If you're dating, and you want to find out how to take it to another level, this book is for you. If you're in a committed relationship, and you want to get the ring, this book is for you. If you're married and you want to regain control and strengthen your bond, or if you're tired of being played with, then I want you to use this book as a tool—to take each of the principles, rules, and tips in this no-nonsense guide and use them to anticipate a man's game plan, and to counter with an offense and defense that's unstoppable. Because trust me: the playbook you all have been using is outdated, and the plays don't work. In fact, the biggest play you have in your arsenal—the one where you walk into a relationship thinking you're going to "change" your man, is the worst and most doomed play of them all. Why? Because no matter what other women are shouting from the covers of magazines, on the television talk shows, during your girlfriend getaway bonding trips, and on blogs from here to Timbuktu, there are basic things in men that are never going to change. No matter how good you are to a man, no matter how good you are for him, until you understand what his makeup is, what drives him, what motivates him, and how he loves, you will be vulnerable to his deception and the games he plays.

But with this book, you can get into a man's mind-set and understand him better, so that you can put into play your plans, your dreams, and your desires, and best of all, you can figure out if he's planning to be with you or just playing with you.

So act like a lady, and think like a man.

PART ONE

The Mind-Set
of a Man

1

WHAT DRIVES MEN

There is no truer statement: men are simple. Get this into your head first, and everything you learn about us in this book will begin to fall into place. Once you get that down, you'll have to understand a few essential truths: men are driven by who they are, what they do, and how much they make. No matter if a man is a CEO, a CON, or both, everything he does is filtered through his title (who he is), how he gets that title (what he does), and the reward he gets for the effort (how much he makes). These three things make up the basic DNA of manhood—the three accomplishments every man must achieve before he feels like he's truly fulfilled his destiny as a man. And until he's achieved his goal in those three areas, the man you're dating, committed to, or married to will be too busy to focus on you.

Think about it: from the moment a boy is born, the first thing everyone around him starts doing is telling him what he must do to be a real man. He is taught to be tough—to wrestle, climb, get up without crying, not let anyone push him around. He is taught to work hard—to do chores around the house, get the groceries out of the car, take out the trash, shovel the snow, cut the grass, and, as soon as he's old enough, get a job. He is taught to protect—to watch out for his mother and his younger siblings, to watch over the house and the family's property. And he is especially encouraged to uphold his family name—make something of himself so that when he walks in a room, everybody is clear about who he is, what he does, and how much he makes. Each of these things is taught in preparation for one thing: manhood.

The pursuit of manhood doesn't change once a boy is grown. In fact, it's only magnified. His focus has always been on, and will remain on, who he is, what he does, and how much he makes until he feels like he's achieved his mission. And until a man does these things, women only fit into the cracks of his life. He's not thinking about settling down, having children, or building a home with anyone until he's got all three of those things in sync. I'm not saying that he has had to have made it, but at least he has to be on track to making it.

This is certainly how it worked for me. I'll never forget how disappointed, frustrated, and unhappy I was when, in my early twenties, I was laid off from the Ford Motor Company. I was already a college dropout, and now, without a job, I hardly had enough money to take care of myself, much less a family. This left me unsure of my future—what I was going to do, how much I was going to make, and what my title would be. The titles "college graduate" and "Ford inspector" were gone; having no job pretty much meant that my chances of bringing home a good paycheck were zero; and I hadn't a clue how I was going to make money. It took me a while to find my footing. I dabbled in various jobs: I owned a carpet cleaning business; I sold carpet; I sold Amway products, the Dick Gregory Bahamian Diet, and ALW Insurance and Commonwealth Insurance. It was madness what I was doing to try to get my life together. Finding someone serious to settle down with was the absolute last thing on my mind.

Then, one night a woman for whom I used to write jokes encouraged me to go to a local comedy club and sign up for amateur night. See, I knew I was funny, and I made a few dollars—very few dollars—writing material for up-and-coming local comedians who were trying to find their way into the industry. But I hadn't a clue, really, how to go about getting into the business for myself. Still, this woman saw something in me and told me to take the stage.

So I did. And I killed. I won $50—which today may not seem like a lot of money, but when I was broke at that time, it felt like $5,000—for telling jokes. I also was guaranteed another fifty dollars if, as the winner, I opened the following week's amateur night competition. The next day, I went to a printer and spent fifteen dollars of my winnings on business cards that, along with my phone number, read: Steve Harvey. Comedian. They were flat and flimsy and didn't have any raised lettering, but those business cards announced that I was Steve Harvey (who I am), and that I had a special talent in comedy (what I do). How much I was going to make remained to be seen, but at least I had the "who I am" and the "what I do" lined up.

If men aren't pursuing their dreams—if we're not chasing the "who we are," the "what we do," and the "how much we make," we're doomed. Dead. But the moment that we figure out the puzzle and feel like our dreams are taking shape, new life breathes into us—it makes us vibrant, enthuses, and animates us. From the moment I became a comedian, I stepped onto that stage ready to be the very best.

Even today, no matter how tired I am, no matter what is going on in my life, I am never late for work, and I've never once missed a gig. Why? Because when I wake up, my dream is in check; I'm living it out live and in color every day, whether it's on the radio during the *Steve Harvey Morning Show,* or on television with my various projects, or onstage, during my *Steve Harvey Live* shows. Who I am is certain—I'm Steve Harvey. What I do is certain: comedy. And how much I make is right in line with what I've always wanted for my family and me.

And now, I can pay attention to my family. All the faux paint in my house, the metal ceilings, the leather chairs, the dogs outside, the cars in the yard, college tuition for my kids—everything is paid for, everyone is set. I can provide for them the way I've always wanted to, I can protect them the way that I was raised to, and in my family's eyes, I am, unquestionably, a man. Which means I have a clear mind when I go to sleep at night.

This is the drive that every man has, whether he's the best player in the NBA, or the best peewee football coach in rural Minnesota; whether he's the head of a Fortune 500 company, or the supervisor on the line at the local bakery; whether he's the kingpin of a major cartel, or the chief corner boy on the block. Encoded in the DNA of the male species is that we are to be the provider and the protector of the family, and everything we do is geared toward ensuring we can make this happen. If a man can afford a place to stay, then he can protect his family from the elements; if he can afford a pair of sneakers for his child, he can feel confident enough to send him or her to school feeling secure and upbeat; if he can afford meat at the grocery store, then he can feel assured that he can feed his family. This is all any man wants; anything less, and he doesn't feel like a man.

Even more, we want to feel like we're number one. We want to be The Best somewhere. In charge. We know we're not going to be head man in every situation, but somewhere in our lives, we're going to be the one everyone answers to because it's that important to us. We want the bragging rights—the right to say, "I'm number one." Women don't seem to care about this so much. But for us men? It's everything. After we've attained that, it's critical that we can show off what we get for being number one. We have to be able to flaunt it, and women have to be able to see it—otherwise, what's the use of being number one?

You need to know this because you have to understand a man's motivation—why he's not home, why he spends so much time working, why he's watching his money the way he does. Because in his world, he's being judged by other men, based on who he is, what he does, and how much he makes. That affects his mood. If you know he's not where he wants to be or not on track for being where he wants to be, then his mood swings at the house will make more sense to you. Your inability to get him to sit and just talk now makes sense. His "on the grind" mentality becomes more clear to you. Really, it's all tied to the three things that drive him.

So if this is on his mind, and he hasn't lined up the who he is, the what he does, and the how much he makes in the way that he sees fit, he can't possibly be to you what he wants to be. Which means that you can't really have the man you want. He can't sit around talking with you, or dream about marriage and family, if his mind is on how to make money, how to get a better position, how to be the kind of man he needs to be for you.

In my experience, these facts don't always sit well with most women. Many of you figure that if a man truly loves you, the two of you should be able to pursue your dreams together. Stability is important to you, but you'd rather build the foundation of your relationship together, no matter the man's station in life. This is honorable, but really, it's not the way men work. His eye will be on the prize, and that prize may not necessarily be you if he isn't up where he wants to be in life. It's impossible for us to focus on the two—we're just not that gifted, sorry.

Mind you, a man doesn't have to make a lot of money right now; as long as he sees his dreams being realized—the title is clear to him, his position is leading him in the direction of the place where he wants to be, and he knows the money will come—then he can rest a little easier, recognizing that he's on the verge of becoming the man he wants to be. The way you can help him get there is to help him focus on his dream, see the vision, and implement his plan. If you can see yourself in that plan (you can get a clearer sense of this in my chapter "The Five Questions Every Woman Should Ask Before She Gets in Too Deep"), then latch on to it. Because when he reaches the level of success he's hoping to reach, he'll be a better, happier man for it—and you will be happy, too.

2

OUR LOVE ISN'T LIKE
YOUR LOVE

Nothing on this planet can compare with a woman's love—it is kind and compassionate, patient and nurturing, generous and sweet and unconditional. Pure. If you are her man, she will walk on water and through a mountain for you, too, no matter how you've acted out, no matter what crazy thing you've done, no matter the time or demand. If you are her man, she will talk to you until there just aren't any more words left to say, encourage you when you're at rock bottom and think there just isn't any way out, hold you in her arms when you're sick, and laugh with you when you're up. And if you're her man and that woman loves you—I mean really loves you?—she will shine you up when you're dusty, encourage you when you're down, defend you even when she's not so sure you were right, and hang on your every word, even when you're not saying anything worth listening to. And no matter what you do, no matter how many times her friends say you're no good, no matter how many times you slam the door on the relationship, she will give you her very best and then some, and keep right on trying to win over your heart, even when you act like everything she's done to convince you she's The One just isn't good enough.

That's a woman's love—it stands the test of time, logic, and all circumstance.

And this is exactly how you all expect us men to love you in return. Ask any woman what kind of love she wants from a man, and it will sound something like this: I want him to be humble and smart, fun and romantic, sensitive and gentle, and, above all, supportive. I want him to look in my eyes and tell me I'm beautiful and that I complete him. I want a man who is vulnerable enough to cry when he's hurting, who will introduce me to his mother with a smile on his face, who loves children and animals, and who is willing to change diapers and wash dishes and do it all without me having to ask. And if he has a nice body and a lot of money and expensive shoes without scuffs, that would be great, too. Amen.

Well, I'm here to tell you that expecting that kind of love—that perfection—from a man is unrealistic. That's right, I said it—it's not gonna happen, no way, no how. Because a man's love isn't like a woman's love.

Don't get it confused, now—I'm not saying that we're not capable of loving. I'm just saying that a man's love is different—much more simple, direct, and probably a little harder to come by. I'll tell you this much: a man who is in love with you is probably not going to call you every half hour and give you an update on how much more he loves you at 5:30 P.M. than he did at 5:00 P.M.; he's not going to sit around stroking your hair and wiping your brow with cold compresses while you sip hot tea and nurse yourself back to health.

His love is still love, though.

It's just different from the love that women give and, in a lot of cases, want.

I argue that if you simply recognize how, exactly, a man loves, you might find that the man standing in front of you is, indeed, giving you his all and then some. How do you know when a man loves you? Simple: he will do each of the following three things.

PROFESS

If your man loves you, he's willing to tell anybody and everybody, "Look, man, this is my woman" or "this is my girl," "my baby's mama," or "my lady." In other words, you will have a title—an official one that far extends beyond "this is my friend," or "this is_____ (insert your name here)." That's because a man who has placed you in the most special part of his heart—the man who truly has feelings for you—will give you a title. That title is his way of letting everyone within the sound of his voice know that he's proud of being with you, and that he has plans for you. He sees himself in a long-term, committed relationship with you, and he's professing it for all to hear because he's serious about this thing—it may be the beginning of something special.

A man who professes you as his own is also saying in not so many words that he's claiming you—that you are his. Now he's put everyone on notice. Any man who hears another man say, "this is my lady," knows that whatever games/tricks/plans/schemes he may have had in mind for the pretty, sexy lady standing in front of him need to be shelved until the next single woman comes in the room, because another man has professed out loud that "this one is mine and she's not available for anything you were plotting and planning." It's a special signal we men all recognize and respect as the universal code for "off-limits."

If he introduces you as his "friend," or by your name, have no doubt that's all you are. He doesn't think any more of you than that. In your heart of hearts, ladies, you all know this. Indeed, when I explained this to a friend of mine, she just laughed and laughed because she could identify with it—saw it up close at an annual Christmas dinner she's been attending with her family and some close friends for going on twelve years. One guy, she said, would show up every year with a new chick—each one prettier than the last—and a new story about his job or his vacation or his new business venture or whatever. While the stories and the women kept changing, the one thing that remained constant was this: none of those women ever got introduced as his girlfriend or lady. They were always, without hesitation, presented by their name. Period. And then he would spend the rest of the night cuddling a hard drink and catching up with old friends and colleagues, leaving her to sit at the table by herself, looking out of place and ridiculous in her fancy dress, trying her best to fit in. Everyone at the table pretty much knew that the moment the couple hit the door and went on their way, none of the regular party attendees would ever see her with him again.

Then one recent Christmas party, he showed up with a new woman—his fingers all intertwined with hers, both of them smiling like Cheshire cats. He introduced her as his "lady," and instantly, everyone knew what was up. But it wasn't just because of the title he'd assigned; it was because of the actions behind it. He was holding her hand, looking directly at her when he talked to her, introducing her around to everyone— from the business folks to his really good friends—running to the bar to get drinks for her, and dancing with her like he didn't want the night to end. And when everyone left that evening,

they all knew they'd be seeing that woman again, fingers intertwined with the hitherto eternal playboy bachelor, one who
changed women as often as Diana Ross changes costumes at a
concert.

And wouldn't you know it? When they came back to that
same function the next year, she had a new title: fiancée. For
sure, she was in this man's plans.

So, if you've been dating a guy for at least ninety days and
you've never met his mother, you don't go to church together,
you haven't been around his family or his friends, and he took you
to a networking/job/social function and introduced you by your
name, then you're not in his plans—he doesn't see you in his future.
But the minute he assigns a title—the moment he lays claim to
you in front of people who mean something to him in his life,
whether it's his boy, his sister, or his boss—that's the minute
you know your man is making a statement. He is professing his
intentions for you—and professing them to the people who
need to know that information. A profession is key—you will
know if a man is serious about you once he claims you.

PROVIDE

Once we've claimed you, and you've returned the honor, we're
going to start bringing home the bacon. Simply put, a man who
loves you will bring that money home to make sure that you and

the kids have what you all need. That is our role—our purpose. Society has told us men for millennium that our primary function is to make sure our families are set—whether we're alive or dead, the people we love need want for nothing. This is the very core of manhood—to be the provider. That's what it's all about. (Okay, there are a few other things; for example, how well you're endowed—and I'm not talking financially—and how well can you provide—now, I am talking financially.) If a man is in a position of being questioned about whether he's able to provide, financially and otherwise, for the ones he loves, you might as well drop-kick his ego into an early grave. The more he can provide for his woman and his kids, the bigger and more alive he feels. Sounds simplistic, but that is the reality.

As a provider, a man pays the bills that have to be paid—the rent, the heat and light bill, the car note; he buys groceries; he pays school tuition; and he takes care of other household expenditures. He will not spend his money on trifling things and come to you with what's left, and he will not selfishly give you a little cut and take the rest for himself. And a man who truly loves you would never make you ask for money for necessities— he would make sure that you need and mostly want for nothing, because every pat on the back he gets for bringing more money into the house, every kiss he gets for handing over cash for school clothes and supplies and toys, every bit of appreciation he gets for keeping the lights and cable on, boosts his prowess as a man. That's why, if he's a real man, he will always put buying something for himself far below his responsibility to provide for his family. His need for another set of golf clubs or expensive shoes or a fancy car or anything else men like to spend their money on will pale in comparison to providing for loved ones, because those golf clubs can't make him square his shoulders the way true appreciation from a woman can. Consequently, everything he does is going to be about trying to make sure the woman he loves has what she needs.

Now I know that expecting a man to care for you financially, no questions asked, in an age in which women have been raised to be financially independent of men gives you pause; if you've been taught all your life to go dutch on your dates and pull out your own checkbook when it comes to paying your bills, and you've been repeatedly told that you can't depend on a man to do anything for you, then it's understandable why you can't wrap your mind around this simple concept. But remember what drives a man; real men do what they have to do to make sure their people are taken care of, clothed, housed, and reasonably satisfied, and if they're doing anything less than that, they're not men—or shall we say, he's not your man, because he will eventually do this for someone's daughter, maybe not you.

For sure, all too many men shirk this responsibility, whether out of selfishness, stupidity, or sheer inability or a combination of all three. But some men simply do not have the education, resources, and wherewithal to make an adequate amount of hard cash. And if a man can't provide, then he doesn't feel like a man, so he flees to escape the horrible feelings of inadequacy, or he's going to bury those feelings in drugs and alcohol. Indeed, you can probably trace a whole host of the pathologies exhibited by the most trifling of men back to their inability to provide. Some try to use crime to make up for it (clearly, our prisons tell us that's not working); some use drugs (our street corners tell us that's not working, either); some just run (the numbers of women raising kids alone, and falling into poverty because of it, tell us that's definitely not working). But ask any one of those men who aren't doing right by themselves or the ones they love what they regret most, and I'll bet you a majority of them will say the same thing: they wish they had the ability to provide.

Of course, some men simply refuse to share the money in their pockets with their women. As some rap songs and hip-hop magazines tell you, these men feel they're being "played" if they provide anything of monetary value to the opposite sex. Some men even label any and every woman who expects her intended to provide for her the very handy, decisively ugly phrase *gold digger*. Oh, when it comes to women, that phrase gets tossed around these days like dough in a New York City pizza parlor. In fact, men have set it up so well that we've got women thinking that if they remotely expect a man to pay for their dinner, or buy them a drink at the bar, or set any financial requirements for their man, then they're gold diggers.

I'm here to tell you, though, ladies, that the term "gold

digger" is one of the traps we men set to keep you off our money trail; we created that term for you so that we can have all of our money and still get everything we want from you without you asking for or expecting this very basic, instinctual responsibility that men all over the world are obligated to assume and embrace. It's a "get-over" term, ladies—one that has a very legitimate premise (there are, of course, women who date and marry men solely for the cold, hard cash), but one that has been wrongly and almost universally applied to any woman who has made clear that she expects her man to fulfill his duty as a man. *Know this: It is your right to expect that a man will pay for your dinner, your movie ticket, your club entry fee, or whatever else he has to pay for in exchange for your time.* You all have to stop this foolishness with the "I pay for my dinner so he knows I don't need him" approach. As I point out in the next chapter, "The Three Things Every Man Needs: Support, Loyalty, and the Cookie," a man—a real one, anyway—wants to feel needed. And the easiest way to help him get that high is to *let* him provide for you. This is only fair.

And if he loves you? Oh, he's going to bring every cent home to you. He's not going to come back from gambling all his money away, saying, "Here's $100—that's all I got this week." He's going to come straight home with that check, and if there's anything left over after he takes care of each and every one of your needs, well, then he'll play. This is man business, baby. It's how we do.

Now, there are different ways to provide besides monetarily. Your man could be broke, but he's going to do everything within his power to make up for this by supplying your needs in other tangible ways. If you're running low on groceries, he may not be able to give you money to go to the store, but he might have a little extra something in his refrigerator and pantry to hold you over until he can give you a couple of dollars. In other words, he's not going to let you go hungry. If your car is broken down, he may not be able to pay for a mechanic, but he can call his buddies over to help him move your ride to the side of the road and give you rides to work until he figures out how to pay for your car to get fixed. If you need some pictures hung, and the sink unclogged, and a new garage door installed, a man who loves you will climb up a twenty-foot ladder to get that picture up on the wall, put a bucket down to catch the overflowing water from the sink while he goes to find the right part he needs to fix the pipes, and pore through the instruction manual for hours to figure out how to get that garage door in. Providing for the ones he loves and cares about, whether it's monetarily or with sweat equity, is a part of a man's DNA, and if he loves and cares for you, this man will provide for you all these things with no limits.

ROTECT

When a man truly loves you, anybody who says, does, suggests, or even thinks about doing something offensive to you stands the risk of being obliterated. Your man will destroy anything and everything in his path to make sure that whoever disrespected you pays for it. This is his nature. You pick most any male species on the planet, and the same is true: no one is going to disrespect their family without paying a cost—or at least putting up a serious fight. This is innate—recognized and respected from the first relationship that a boy has, that relationship being with his mother. He may not know what unconditional love is yet, but a boy child will never (a)admit that his mother is capable of making mistakes, or (b) let someone say or do something to his mother. This is taught to males practically from the womb—cover your mother, protect her, don't let anybody say anything about her or do anything to her, and if they do, let them know it's time to take it outside. This is most certainly the way it was taught in my house, too. I remember distinctly when I was a little boy, probably around age eight or so, standing there waiting for my mother to pull on her coat for our bus ride downtown. My father came in the room and said, very simply, "You and your mother are going downtown—watch out for your mother." That was rule number one in my father's house: Do not come back in this house without your mother and your sisters. You might as well kill yourself or get on a bus and go somewhere else, but don't come back without your mother and the girls. Now, I knew good and hell well that if anybody so much as raised a finger to my mother, I wouldn't be able to do anything about it—that she was really taking care of me on that bus. But, buddy, I'd be on the bus and in the store with my little chest stuck out, swearing I was doing something to protect my family.

Because that was what I was supposed to do.

Indeed, that is what every man is supposed to—and is willing to do—for the people for whom he professes and provides. Once he says he cares about you, you are a prized possession to him, he will do anything to protect that prized possession. If he's hearing you argue with a bill collector, he's going to say, "Who are you talking to? Let me talk to him right quick." If your ex is calling and bringing drama in your life, your man is going to talk to him about it. If he sees your kids are cutting up and getting out of hand, he's going to talk to them, too. In other words, he's going to be providing protection and leadership for his family because he knows a real man is a protector. There is not a real man living who will not protect what is his. It's about respect.

I'd argue that this is most certainly one of the key things any woman wants in her man, because it is what girls have been raised to expect—that they can count on the most important men in their lives to go to battle for them, and keep them safe from all harm, no matter the cost. I think you all know this so well that you take great care in letting a man who loves you know when someone's been a threat or danger to you, because you know that your man—whether he be your father, brother, uncle, husband, or lover—is going to do everything in his power and then some to defend your honor. Maybe even hurt somebody, despite the consequences. For instance, you probably don't really want to hype what's going on down at your job because he might head down to the job and have a few words with your boss if necessary. And we all know that would not be a good situation.

I remember one time when my mother was at home and the insurance man came by looking for some money my mother didn't have. My father was at work, so he didn't actually witness this man come to our front door and say to my mother, "The next time I come here, you better have this money or else." My dad got wind of the situation from one of my siblings, and when he asked my mother what, exactly, this man said to her, she hesitated and hemmed and hawed for a long time before she finally broke down and told my father about the exchange. She didn't really want to tell him what went down because she knew my father would snap. When he finally had the information he needed, my father came to me and asked what time the insurance man usually shows up, and I told him. And the next time that man came by the house, my father was there waiting for him. I'll never forget the image; that man never made it past the back of his car. When we looked out the window, my father had that man bent over the car with both his hands on that man's neck. "If you ever say anything disrespectful to my wife again, I will *kill* you," he said. Now, that may seem a little extreme, but this is what real men do to protect the ones they love.

Protection isn't just about using brute, physical force against someone, though. A man who truly cares about or loves you can and will protect you in other ways, whether it be with advice, or stepping up to perform a task that he thinks is too dangerous for you to do. For instance, if it's dark outside, he may not want you to put the car in the driveway or walk the dog by yourself because he fears for your safety; in this instance, he'll move the cars and walk the dog himself, even if he's just off a double shift, so that you can be inside where it's safe. If you're walking by someone who looks like he might be a threat, a man who loves you is going to protect you by putting himself between you and that guy as you walk by so if he tries anything, he'll have to get through your man before he so much as lays a finger on you.

My wife, Marjorie, still cracks up when she thinks about how I "protected" her on a recent joint fishing and diving trip we took in Maui. See, my wife is a certified scuba diver. I am not. When we got out on those choppy waters of the Pacific Ocean, I couldn't help but feel like something was going to happen to my wife down there, and I wouldn't have any way of protecting her. Nonetheless, she put on all the equipment and began to descend into the water. I got antsy and immediately started lighting up cigars and walking around the boat explaining to the dive masters that "this one has to come back." By the time she was actually under the water, I'd told my security guy, who can't scuba dive, to put on his snorkel and get in and keep an eye on her. I'd also told everyone onboard—from my manager to the captain—that "if my wife is not back up here in thirty-five minutes, everybody's putting on some suits and we're going to go get her." The guy leading the expedition said as nicely as he could, "Sir, everybody can't go down to save one person," but his words meant nothing to me. "I'm telling you," I said, getting a little more jumpy with each word, "Either everybody goes down there to save her, or I'm killing everybody on the boat. This boat goes nowhere without her, and if it pulls off and she's not on it, that's it for everybody."

My wife must have sensed something was up because suddenly, she was back above water. She knew that I was acting up. And rather than dive, she returned to the boat, because she knew how nervous I was about the whole idea of her submerged under water where I couldn't act on my natural instincts to protect her; she figured it was better to sit that dive out. She understands that primal need I have to make sure nothing bad happens to her. Marjorie is a pretty adventurous girl, but she's cut out a lot of that stuff—the diving and parasailing and such—for that very reason. I finally get the woman of my dreams and while she's out having fun the parachute wire jams and next thing I know she's flying into walls, or she's diving and the scuba tank doesn't work? Her life is in jeopardy and I can't do anything about it? No sir. Nope. No more of that. My philosophy for having a good time is that you have to have a good time and return home in one piece so you can tell everybody about your good time. My wife doesn't trip about this; she just says, "Thanks for caring, honey."

And I do care about her, so my DNA screams out to me to protect her and provide for her and profess about her in any way that I can. This, by the way, is how our fathers did it, and their fathers, and their fathers, too—to the best of their natural ability and with the help of God, even in the most adverse times when protecting and providing and even professing were neither easy nor, in the case of black men, allowed. We've lost sight of this—stopped demanding it from our men. Maybe it's because there are so many women left to raise their children alone, or maybe it's because there just haven't been enough men teaching our boys how to be true men. But I firmly believe that a real woman can bring out the best in a man; sometimes we need only meet a real woman other than our own mother to bring out our best qualities. That, however, requires something of the woman; she's got to demand that every man stand and deliver. On the radio show and in my everyday interactions with my colleagues and friends, I constantly hear women say that there aren't any good men and complain about all the things men won't do.

But I contend they don't do the things that real men are expected to do because no one—especially, women—*requires* it of them (see my chapter "Men Respect Standards—Get Some").

*I*n sum, ladies, you have to stop heaping your own definition of love on men and recognize that men love differently. A man's love fits only into three categories. As I've explained, I call them "The Three Ps of Love—Profess, Provide, and Protect." A man may not go shopping with you to buy the new dress for your office party, but a real man will escort you to that party, hold your hand, and proudly introduce you all around the party as his lady (profess); he may not cuddle you and sit by the bed holding your hand while you're sick, but a real man who loves you will make sure the prescription is filled, heat up a can of soup, and make sure everybody is in position until you are better (provide); and he may not willingly change diapers, wash the dishes, and rub your feet after a hot bath, but a real man who loves you sure will walk through a mountain and on water before he'd let someone bring any hurt or harm to you (protect). This much you can believe.

If you've got a man who does these things for you, trust me, he's all in.

3

THE THREE THINGS
EVERY MAN NEEDS

Support, Loyalty, and the Cookie

W omen are complicated creatures. You need stuff. Lots of it. And you expect your man to provide it, even if you haven't explained what it is you need and want, or even if what you needed and wanted five minutes ago is wholly different from what you need and want now. In fact, I've said over and over again jokingly that the only way a woman can truly be completely satisfied is to get herself four different men—an old one, an ugly one, a Mandingo, and a gay guy. Now the four of them combined? They got you covered.

The old man—he'll sit around the house with you, spend his pension check on you, hug you, hold you, give you comfort, and won't expect any sex from you because, well, he can't get it up no way. From him, you get financial security. The ugly one? He'll go above and beyond the call of duty to help you out: he'll take the kids to their lessons after school, run you down to the grocery store, wash the car on the weekends, babysit the cat—whatever you need, he'll provide it because he's just happy someone as beautiful as you is paying him any kind of attention. From him, you get "me time." He frees you up to do all the things you need time to do. And then there's the Mandingo man. You need a big ol' Mandingo man. You know what you gonna get from him. He's big, he's not that smart, can't hold a good conversation, got muscles popping out from his eyebrows to his pinkie toe and when you see him, you know he's going to put your back out. That's all you want from him, and he makes sure he gives it to you real good. Mind-blowing sex—that's what you get from Mandingo. And then you need a gay guy—someone you can go shopping with, who doesn't want anything from you but gossip and details about what the old man bought you, which errands you sent the ugly guy to take care of, and exactly how Mandingo had you doing monkey flips for a week. See, the gay guy gives you all the conversation you need (smile).

Four guys, supplying each of your needs *should* bring you happiness. I say should because for women, happiness isn't guaranteed, even once their needs have been met. We fully recognize that you maintain the right to change at any time the perimeters, conditions, and specifics of what, exactly, will make you happy, and we try to adjust accordingly, and usually can't.

Now men, by contrast, are very simple creatures. It really doesn't take much to make us happy. In fact, there are only three things that pretty much every man needs—support, love, and "The Cookie." Three things—that's it. And I'm here to tell you that yes, *it's that simple.* What we need never weakens or wavers—hardly ever gets more demanding or harder to achieve. In fact, I'd argue that it's easy for a woman to give her man support, love, and sex because it's in her makeup—support and love are things that women dole out innately and freely. You just call it something else: nurturing. And if you love a man enough to nurture him, then I'd argue you love him enough to be intimate with him. So those three things come natural to you. And this is all your man wants from you. Let me break it down.

NEED #1 Your Support.

We have to feel like somebody's got our back—like we're the king, even if we're not. You have to understand that when we walk out the door, the entire world is standing at the ready to beat us down. Black, white, yellow, striped, every man leaves the house ready to battle. He might have a job where three people can walk by his desk and give him a pink slip at any given moment—change his life in the flash of an eye. The guy in the position beneath your man's may be just searching for a way to undermine him, so he can get the bigger pay—and he doesn't give a damn about whether what he says and does can put your man's job in jeopardy. Your man could be driving down the street minding his own business and get pulled over and something could happen that he has no control over, or someone may try to come and take what he's got. In other words, a man is constantly on the lookout, sizing up the next man, standing at the ready to defend his and all of his gains (that would include you).

So when we walk back in our house, we want to be able to let our guard down. All we want, really, is to hear you say, "Baby, how was your day? Thank you for making it happen for us. This family needs you and wants you and is happy to have you." We've got to feel like we're king, even if we don't act kingly. Trust me, the more you make us feel like we're special, the more we'll give in return. We'll just try harder. Plain and simple. Take a page from my mother: every Sunday morning, my daddy cut my hair for church, and when I got out of that chair, and lotioned up and put on my suit and my shoes and walked into the living room where my mother was waiting for me, she would take one look at me and say, "Look at that boy's haircut—boy, you clean!" or "Look at you, boy—you sharp when you go to church!" I internalized the message—if I got a fresh haircut and I put on a nice suit, my mother would compliment me, and I would walk out of the house with my shoulders squared and head held high because my mother said I looked good and she was encouraging me to be presentable. And my father's chest was out as far as mine because every Sunday, she reminded him that he made it all possible; she kissed and thanked him every Sunday.

A man needs that from his woman—he needs her to say, "Baby, I can't tell you how much I appreciate what you do for me and the kids." Those simple words give us the strength to keep on doing right by you and the family. From working harder on the job, to bringing home that paycheck, to something as simple as throwing some meat on the grill on Saturday evenings or folding up a load of the laundry, we'll do it more often if there is reward in it. That reward doesn't cost you one red penny. It simply comes from the heart: *Thank you, baby. I appreciate you.* You don't know how important that is for your man; that little bit of encouragement makes him want to do more. You think because we're hard and we don't want to cuddle that we don't need that encouragement, but we do. And the woman who comes along and says, "You so big and strong and you're everything I need," well, we're going to go get some more of that!

NEED #2   **Your Loyalty.**

Please understand that our love is wholly different from a woman's love. A woman's love is emotional, nurturing, heart-felt—sweet and kind and all encompassing. You can slice a knife through it, it's so thick. And when she's in love with you, she is loyal to you—she can't see herself with someone else, because for her, no one else will do. That's a woman's love.

But for men, love is loyalty. We want you to show your love to us by being loyal. That means that no matter what, you're going to stand beside us. We get laid off, we know you're going to stay, even if we're not drawing a paycheck. You get around your girlfriends, you're going to say with great enthusiasm, "That's *my* man. I'm loyal to *him*." Idris Elba, Denzel, Usher, or the like walks into the room, money dripping from their suit jacket, floating on air and glistening and all that? You're going to hold on to our hand a little tighter and say from the bottom of your heart, "I don't want any of those shiny, rich, fine men because my man is the only one for me!" (We can only hope that's what you'll say—smile.)

That's loyalty—our kind of love. To men, they are one and the same. The kind of love you require is beautiful, but our love isn't like your love. It's different, though it's still love. And a man's love is a very powerful thing. It's amazing love. If your loyalty is real and unimpeachable, that man will kill concrete for you. He ain't going no damn where.

NEED #3   ## The Cookie.

No-brainer. Men. Need. Sex. We love it. Ain't nothin' on this planet like it, nothing else we want that bad on a continuous basis, nothing else we simply cannot live without. Take our house, take our job, the '69 Impala, our last pair of gators, but please—puh-leeze—don't hold out on the cookie. We don't care about anything else; we need the cookie. We need to be physically engaged with the woman we love, the woman who is loyal to us and supports us, and the way that we do that is by making love. The emotional stuff—the talking, the cuddling, the holding hands, and bonding, that's y'all's thing. We'll do those things because we know it's important to you. But please understand: the way we men connect is by having sex. Period. It's how we plug in, recharge, and reconnect. I don't know of a man who doesn't need this. Ask any guy if sex is important in a relationship and the one who says no is lying. I just haven't met that guy yet. When you meet him, let's get him in to the Smithsonian—he's that special and rare. But the rest of us men? We need sex like we need air.

You got about a good month at best without it. And then he's going to get it from somewhere else (unless you're carrying his child). I'm telling you: gangs are built on support and loyalty; dudes go out and form gangs built on those two things right there. The only thing missing is sex, and that's where the girl gang members come in. It's the same thing with motorcycle clubs, the country club, the Elks, the Masons, frats—the whole of a man's world is built on these three principles. There's not one day of the week that we are not waking up in the pursuit of it. Let's say you're *not* a member of Alpha Phi Alpha, Kappa Alpha Psi, or you're an almighty member of Omega Psi Phi, and someone who hasn't pledged their undying support and love to frat on a line for at least six weeks—be that person putting on their colors and let them find out you haven't pledged, that you didn't cross over. Do you know what the hell would happen if those boys found out you're not frat? Messing with their loyalty—their colors? Man, not nary a day. Be a Crip and go to a Blood's house and see what happens. Try going into that country club and you're not a member. Loyalty. Support. That's what men are made of.

And can't one of them survive without sex. Oh, he'll work with you if you have an off week—if he loves you, that is. If he didn't care, he wouldn't bother to try to get your cookie—he'd just go on and get it from somewhere else. But if he's into you, and you're cutting back, rationing it out, you're not doing what you did when you all first started dating, he's going to line up someone who will. Please believe me when I tell you this: he will tell everybody, "This is my girl right here," but meanwhile, he will have another woman lined up and waiting to give him what he needs and wants—the cookie.

Don't get it wrong—we're not animals. We know things change, the baby comes and the doctor says we have to wait six weeks, or your monthly is on the way, your hormones are acting up and you're not in the mood. But the excuses can't go on forever. You can play your man short if you want to. No matter how much a man loves his wife, his family, his house, his role as the man of the house, the one who's bringing in all the money into family account, maybe even putting a little extra into yours, if you mess around and start shelling out the cookie in crumbs, it's going to be a problem.

Speaking of my own experience, I recently turned fifty and I'm telling you right now, don't play me short in this area. At my age, I'll work with you for a little longer, because I'm busy, I got a company to run, I got a schedule to keep, I'm on the road, on the stage, on the radio, writing books, acting, supporting my own charity and working with others. I'm on the run. And at my age, I can't afford to mess up—mentally, emotionally, or spiritually. Hell is no longer an option for me. I'm doing what I can to get to the Gate, and it could be any day now. If I start messing around, I might have a stroke and miss out on my homegoing. But the truth is, if I can't go home and relieve my stress, there is a problem. If I've talked to the Lord and tried to get you motivated to give me some of the cookie and you're still coming up with reasons why you just can't be intimate with me, something is going to change.

And I'm ready to bet things aren't so different in your household. You might have been up all night for a week with a sick child, gotten up early to get the other onto the school bus before you hit the road for that rush-hour commute to work, gone to battle with your co-workers and boss for eight hours with nothing but a fifteen-minute break to swallow an inadequate, unsatisfying lunch, and then hit the rush-hour traffic back home to start your second job—the feeding and care of your kids. There's dinner to be cooked, and homework to be checked, and laundry to be done, and the list goes on. By the time your man checks in with you, the last thing on your mind is giving a positive response to what a friend of mine called "the shoulder tap." "You know what I'm talking about," she said. "It's when you finally drop into the bed exhausted, and you're halfway through your favorite show you watch when you just want to zone out, and here he comes, tapping you on your shoulder, asking for sex. It's just annoying."

What that same friend of mine didn't know, though, was that her husband was tired of the "shoulder tap," too. In his mind, he'd also worked all day—just as hard as her. And though he may not have done all the exact things she'd done during the course of the evening at home, he, too, put in work around the house, and, like her, needed to wind down from his day. She liked watching television. He liked to have sex. She was always too tired to have sex. He was tired of not having sex. So while she unwound to her favorite shows, he unwound out of the house—with another woman.

Now, I'm not saying what he did was right. But as a man, I can understand the logic behind what he eventually ended up doing. And if I were in their bedroom before all of the ugliness from his cheating ways went down, I would have given them what I've found to be some very sage advice: acknowledge the ones you love. That means that if a man sees his woman had a hard day and she could stand some more help around the house to make the evenings go more smoothly, her man needs to step up his game. If she cooks, he does the dishes. If she gets the kids' clothes ready for tomorrow, he gets their homework ready for tomorrow. If she gets the kids off to bed, he gets his wife off in bed by setting the mood—straightening up, running her a bath, letting her settle in with a glass of wine, whatever it takes to make it clear to her that having sex with the woman he loves is not only a release, but an act of love. And she, perhaps, will be more willing to reciprocate—not with annoyance, but with the sheer giddiness in knowing how it feels to feel wanted.

But understand that no man is going to wine and dine his wife every night in order to have sex with her. That's unreasonable. Sometimes, he's just going to want to have you, no frills—without being forced to feel like he's added another "chore" to your list of things to do. Every man needs that from his woman. Every last one of us.

To sum up, we've got to have these three things—support, loyalty, and sex—from you or we're going to go. You can shop for us, cook dinner every night, and make sure our favorite peanut butter is in the cabinet to show us that you're paying attention and you care. But what we really need from you when our day goes bad is those three things. You give me that when I come home, and I'll go back out there and fight this war for you. The moment a woman isn't doing those three things for her man, I can promise you he'll get somebody who will. We cannot survive without these things—not for ninety days, we can't.

You may not like what I'm saying, but ask any man about these words and whether they're true, and that man will tell you this one simple thing: it's true. Support. Loyalty. The cookie. If you supply these three things, you'll have on your hands a man who will do anything you need and want him to do for you—pure and simple.

4

"WE NEED TO TALK,"
AND OTHER WORDS THAT MAKE
MEN RUN FOR COVER

We need to talk."

For a man, few words are as menacing as those four—especially when a woman is the one saying them and he's on the receiving end. Those four words can mean only two things to men: either we did something wrong or, worse, you really literally just want to talk. Now, we understand that we're not the essence of perfection and there are going to be times when you're mad at us and need to let us know it; we get that, though we don't necessarily want to have to concentrate on an hourlong angry lecture about how we screwed up. But even more? No man wants to sit around gabbing with you like we're one of your girlfriends. Ever. It's just not in our DNA to lounge around, sip coffee, and dab at our eyes with tissue as if we're in an AA meeting or on some psychologist's couch trying to get things off our chest. When men are talking, and especially when they're listening, it's with purpose.

We don't vent.

We just want to fix whatever situation is upsetting the balance.

We understand that this frustrates you time and time again, because sometimes you want to talk to share and get someone else's take on a situation—you know, put a listening ear on it. But seriously? That's what your girlfriends are for. You lay out your problem and she'll commiserate with you—give you all kinds of "yeah, girls" and "I know that's right," and nod and agree and tell you stories about how the same thing happened to her. She'll even go on to give you concrete examples of every other time something like this has happened to other women throughout the history of the world, and, hours later, you all will get up from the couch, having solved nothing but feeling so much better. Consider Exhibit A:

> **You:** "I walked into work today and before I could get to my desk, I saw Tanya walking over to the coffee machine and wouldn't you know that heiffa had on the same shirt as me?"
>
> **Your girlfriend:** "You better stop it. Which one?"

You: "The blue one—you know, the one with the orange flower print? I got it from that store across town? On sale?"

Your girlfriend: "You mean the one you found on the $29.99 rack in the back? The same day I found those shoes at the store just down the street?"

You: "That's the one! I wore that shirt to work a few weeks ago and she complimented me on it and next thing I know, she ran to the store and bought my shirt and is wearing it to work! Can you believe it? Do you know how that made me feel?"

Your girlfriend: "Aw, hell to the nah. Are you serious? That's horrible. She's got some nerve . . ."

For sure, this conversation could go on for hours, morphing into all kinds of side conversations that have absolutely nothing to do with the issue at hand: that some woman was wearing the same blouse as you on the same day in the same office.

With a man, exactly ten seconds into the conversation, he'd arrive at The Fix. I present to you, Exhibit B:

You: "I walked into work today and before I could get to my desk, I saw Tanya walking over to the coffee machine and wouldn't you know that heiffa had on the same shirt as me?"

Your man: "Really? Don't wear it anymore."

End of conversation. It's that simple for us. In this particular instance, and many more examples such as this, we can't get more worked up than that. How you felt at work while you had to sit there with this other woman on the other side of the room with the same blouse on is irrelevant to us. As far as we're concerned, the problem has already been fixed—you came home. You're not looking at the woman in the identical blouse anymore. And if you don't wear that particular blouse to the office again, you won't have to deal with that particular problem again. In our mind, problem solved—no more talking.

All of this is to say that we men aren't in the talking business; we're in the fix-it business. From the moment we come out of the womb, we're taught to protect, profess, and provide. Communicating, nurturing, listening to problems, and trying to understand them without any obligation to fix them is simply not what boys are raised to do. We don't let them cry, we don't ask them how they feel about anything, we don't encourage them to express themselves in any meaningful way beyond showing how "manly" they are. Let a little boy fall off his bike and scrape his knee—see how fast everyone tells him to get up and shake it off and stop all that doggone crying. "Be a man," we demand. There's no discussion about how he felt when he hit the ground—nobody's asking him to talk about whether he's too scared to get back on the bike and try again. Our automatic response is to tell him to get over it, get back on the bike, and figure out how to ride it so he doesn't fall again.

Now that he's grown and in a relationship, you expect that same boy who was told to keep quiet and keep it moving to be a man who can sit and listen and communicate and nurture? I'm telling you now: your expectations are off. Women have different moods, and ideas in their head, and you all expect us to fall in line, and if we don't, it's a problem—you're telling your girlfriends, "He won't talk to me," and "I can't get him to open up." But opening up is not what we do. Profess, provide, and protect—all our lives, that's what we men have been taught and encouraged to do. This, we've been told, is how a man shows his love. And The Fix falls firmly into the "provide" category. For sure, provision isn't just about money; for us, providing also is about righting what's wrong, and figuring out what's going to keep everybody happy. Because any man with sense knows that when mama's happy, we're all going to be happy. And when you're happy, there is a great return for us. So we provide and fix.

I'm telling you right now: if you go to your man with a situation that's fixable and he doesn't try to fix it, he is not your man—he is not in love with you. Go ahead, I dare you to try it for yourself. When your man comes over, tell him, "You know,

I just can't stand this kitchen this way. The color just throws me all off, the cabinets are all wrong, they don't go with the stove and I can't get my mind right in here when I'm trying to cook." If he's all the way in it with you, he will say, without hesitation, "What color you want this kitchen to be, baby?" Tell him "pink," and see if by next Saturday the whole kitchen isn't painted pink, cabinets and all. He will see your distress, understand that if you don't like the cabinets and the walls and the way the stove functions, you're going to walk into that kitchen with your mouth poked out—phoning in the home-cooked meals because you just can't hook up the steaks and baked potatoes like you want to in a kitchen you can't stand. And we definitely don't want that, so to the hardware store we will go. Even if we don't have money for a complete remodel, we'll go and find you some hardware for the cabinets, maybe some new handles, and some sandpaper—lots of sandpaper—to get that color you can't stand off your cabinets, so that we can refinish them exactly the way you want them to be finished. A man who really loves you can't wait to do this for you, because in the back of his mind, he can envision you with a smile on your face, setting his place at the head of the table, and serving up a fine meal in the new kitchen he fixed just for you. (Oh, make no mistake about it: we want to see you happy, but it's also all about the return, ladies. Please understand and respect the return.)

Of course, we operate under the assumption that The Fix

isn't always going to be on point. We stay off balance because even though we're responding in a way that we believe is logical, our women will inevitably respond emotionally—which always throws a monkey wrench right into the middle of what we're trying to accomplish. Most of the time, it feels to us that your response is determined not wholly by what is rational, but mostly by how you're feeling that particular day, at that particular moment. A perfect example: your man can lick you on the same breast with the same amount of moisture in the same exact position that had you hollering and screaming last night, and this evening, you will look at him and say, with conviction, "What are you doing? I don't want that." And now he's all confused because, hey, if you lick him on that spot and he liked it yesterday, he's going to like it today and tomorrow and the day after that, too. But you, not so much. What you like and how you like it seemingly shifts from day to day, sometimes even moment to moment. And that is not logical to us—we can't figure it out, ever. If we get it right, great. But sometimes, we're just going to get it wrong. A lot of times, the more inexperienced of us men are going to completely screw it up. For example, consider a woman who walks into the room in a visible huff; a guy who's young and not too smart in this relationship business may ask his lady what's wrong, and she may say, "nothing." That fool will be the one to say, "Okay, cool." He will also be the one who gets laid out with the, "Dammit—you saw me tripping and you're just going to walk off without seeing about me?" Yup, that guy is going to have a lot of fixing to do.

But the more experienced man—the one who can read his lady's moods and tell when something is wrong—is going to ask her what's up, and no matter how many times she says, "nothing," he's going to ask again and again until she starts coming clean and opens up, though, in his heart of hearts, he will be hoping to God there's really nothing wrong, and if there is something wrong, he will be able to just fix it because he doesn't want to see her pout. Even when he thinks she is done talking, he'll push her until the issue is resolved because he can't leave it at, "Wow, sorry that happened." He will immediately launch into The Fix.

This is not to say you'll never have a conversation with your man that lasts longer than two minutes. We understand that sometimes we're going to have to give a little more in terms of communicating with you—that every now and then we're going to have to spill our guts and reveal what's going on in our heads. We also know that you may just want to lie in our arms and cuddle and talk it out with absolutely no resolution. We are capable of doing this, too. It's not easy. But it can be done. We know that sitting and listening and even participating in a long conversation about your feelings is necessary and inevitable. But don't be surprised if those conversations are few and far between. Detailed conversation is what you have with your girlfriends. Men just want to hear the problem and then fix it. It's about maintaining this balance—the two of you understanding exactly what each other requires to be innately happy, and then trying to provide at least some of that so that both mates feel like they're in this relationship with the other. For men, that means that every once in a while, they may have to sit and be still and just listen. For women, it would go a long way if they respected the encryption of manhood—that we're too focused on who we are, what we do, and how much we make to spend a whole lot of time sitting around pondering things that can't be fixed.

Of course, it would go a long way if women stopped opening the conversation with "we need to talk." The moment you say that, our defenses go up, the repair tools come out, the sweat starts rolling, and we're sprinting through the events of the past weeks, trying to figure out what we did wrong, when we did it, and how we're going to fix it so that we're not in trouble anymore.

In fact, I think it's a good idea that, if you just want to vent, you start the conversation with something simple, like, "Honey, look, nothing is really wrong—I just want to tell somebody something." That's a great opening line; it allows us to relax, take our foot down from the witness stand, put away our "fix it" tools, and actually sit and listen to what you have to say.

PART TWO

Why Men Do What They Do

5

FIRST THINGS FIRST

He Wants to Sleep with You

We were doing the *Steve Harvey Morning Show* live by remote in Detroit, and a woman came up to the podium to say hello to me and the crew—a really attractive girl, nicely dressed, with beautiful dark skin, pretty white teeth, gorgeous body, really put together all around. And when she started talking, she really threw me because I could hear in her voice that she was mature, but she just didn't look like she sounded. So I asked the lady how old she was; she said she was forty-two. Blew me away. I didn't think she was a day older than thirty. Then I asked her how many kids she had. "Five," she said, smiling from ear to ear. "I've got three of my own, and I adopted two."

Now I'm sitting here thinking, wow—that's really slick. She's over age forty, she's taking care of not only the kids she gave birth to, but two more she took in out of the kindness and generosity of her heart, and she looks years younger than she really is—she's really got it going on. Be clear: I wasn't about to do anything with this information because guess what? I'm a happily married man—emphasis on happily. But some years ago, that conversation would have gone down a wholly different way, and it would not have involved me asking her anything about her kids, where she works, how she's living—none of that.

But a guy who was all in her space while we continued doing our show—that's another story. He clearly had plans for this lady. You could tell just by the way he was leaning into her, hanging on her every word. Oh, he was talking to her like there weren't hundreds of people surrounding them—like my cohost and I weren't in the middle of a show. I knew what he was trying to get to. But clearly, *she* had no clue.

In front of everyone during a commercial break, I asked her, "What does *he* want?"

She laughed and gave me a confused look. "Nothing," she giggled. "We're just making small talk." Mind you, the guy trying to talk to her isn't saying a word. He knows that I know. And after a few more commercial breaks, and a lot more of his obvious moves, I finally told her he was looking for much more than a simple conversation.

"He wants something from you," I said. "I can prove it to you."

Now the crowd, full of mostly women, is goading me on. "Here's the deal," I said. "Turn around right now, look in his face, and do not take your eyes off his eyes. Now tell him how many kids you got and watch his reaction."

The man seemed calm until she got to the word *five*. He reeled back like a spooked horse; his whole facial structure changed, and even though he covered his mouth, he couldn't keep his surprised, "Ooh," from escaping his lips.

He couldn't get away from her fast enough. The next break, he was down on the other end of the venue—fifty feet away, in some other woman's face. See, he wanted something from her, but that something didn't include five kids. He had a good job, he appeared intelligent. He had told me he was making good money; clearly, however, he couldn't foresee his money split those many ways. When he was flirting with this woman, all he envisioned was he and her getting down to it, no strings attached.

My cohost just laughed and laughed and asked me how I knew all of this. It's easy: when a man approaches you, he has a plan. And the main plan is to sleep with you, or to find out what it takes to sleep with you.

Here's a generalization but in my experience, it's true. Women love to sit and talk for no apparent reason but to talk, but we men, we're just not cut out to chitchat for the sake of chitchat—we don't have time for it. We men are very simple people: if we like what we see, we're coming over there. If we don't want anything from you, we're not coming over there. Period. Please highlight this part right here so you can always remind yourself the next time a man steps to you: a man always wants something. *Always*. And when it comes to women, that plan is always to find out two things: (1) if you're willing to sleep with him, and (2) if you are, how much it will cost to get you to sleep with him.

That's his mission in the club.

That's his charge in the lunchroom at the office.

That's what he's up to when he skips past all those seats at the church and sits down in the pew right next to you.

If a man sees you and asks you how you're doing, what do you think he came over there for? He didn't come over to learn anything from you, to find out about your interests and likes and wants. That's what women do when they're interested in getting to know someone. For a man, it's really less complicated: he liked what he saw from across the room and now he's going to go over there and get it. He doesn't care anything about your personality or what you do for a living; your friends mean nothing to him, and whether you know Jesus is irrelevant. He just wants to know if he might be able to sleep with you, and he's talking to you to determine exactly how much he has to invest to get what he wants.

When I say, "invest," I'm not talking solely about monetary

values; I'm talking about your values—your requirements. He's trying to see if your "price" is too high, if it's affordable, if he can get it on credit, whether he can get it tonight. If you don't lay out any requirements, then you're free—game on. He knows he can get you to the bed with minimal effort. But if you tell him up front you have requirements—that you need his time, his respect, his attention—then he knows you're expensive, that he's going to need to put in work to get the cookie. For some men, that cost may be too high—they're just looking for a good time and have no interest in "investing" time and respect and a commitment. One man may assess right away, "Man, I got to go by there two or three times a week, gas is five dollars a gallon, I got this other woman I'm hollering at, I'm going to have to call her and all of that. No, that price is out of my range." For another man, your sticker price may be affordable.

This is useful information to you because now you know when a man approaches you, you can cut through the riffraff, lay down your requirements (which I'll talk about later), and determine right away whether he's willing to pay for what it is he's looking for. Okay, so ladies: it's no secret now—and you can act accordingly. When you're not aware that all men have plans, you're not placing requirements on him, and if you're not setting any ground rules, then you're essentially telling him that you're open for *his* rules. You've established that you don't care how often he calls, when he comes by, how often you all talk, and whether he opens your door; this means that he'll call you when he gets ready, he won't be opening any of your doors, and even though you asked him to be there at seven, he won't show up until eight—all because you didn't (a) acknowledge that a man always has a plan and (b) act accordingly.

This is precisely what was on my father-in-law's mind when one of my daughters brought home her alleged "boyfriend" to the house for a family dinner. You should know that my father-in-law is one of the smartest men I ever met in my life—he's a man I look up to, and I look up to very few men. The things that come out of his mouth are usually, if not always, on point and make me think. The same was true this particular evening when he lined up this boy on the living room couch and asked him plain as day, "So, what's your plan with my granddaughter?"

The young man, about thirty, asked very simply, "What do you mean by that?"

"I mean just what I asked," my father-in-law said. "What is your plan?"

"I don't have no plan," he said.

"Then what are you doing?" my father-in-law asked.

"I'm just trying to get to know her," he insisted.

"But what's your plan? Where is this going?" my father-in-law snapped back.

Finally, under the pressure of the questioning, the squared shoulders, and two straight-faced black men making it clear we know the game, the boy finally broke down and said those four fateful words: "We're just kicking it."

My father-in-law sat there and stared at him for a minute, satisfied, finally, that he'd gotten to the bottom of it. He tasted blood. "Okay, then—cool," my father-in-law said quietly. "Let's share that with her, that you're just 'kicking it.' Let's see how she feels being the kicked one. Let's take that back to her."

She looked so crazy when, a few minutes later, we let her know about her man's plans—that they're just "kicking it." Because she knows from our constant talks and updates and sessions about men that when it comes to relationships, you're either being kicked or you're potential long-term material. It can't be both. Clearly, he had a plan that was different from what she wanted.

Luckily my daughter had her granddad and me to help her decipher her man's plan. But not every woman has a father figure around to hip her to the game. Now, when that man comes smiling all up in your face and talking like he's really into you, act like you know. Because now, you do: he wants to sleep with you.

What's your price?

If you let him know up front, he will let you know up front if it's too high a price for him to pay. And then you can move on.

6

❦ ❧

SPORTS FISH VS. KEEPERS

How Men Distinguish Between the Marrying Types and the Playthings

Anyone who really knows me knows about my passion for fishing. I've always loved the tranquil moments that come with the sport—sitting on the bank or the deck of a boat, out on the open water. There is no greater peace. But I also crave the sudden explosion of adrenaline that comes when I feel a fish on the other end of my line; you can't imagine the thrill that comes when I have to use every bit of my might and mind to see if I can keep this fish hooked, reel it in, and get it in the boat.

And then comes the hard part—deciding whether to keep the fish or throw it back. So in addition to fishing, hooking them, and reeling them in, I get another rush when I'm forced to look at them, see how they feel, and evaluate whether they make it on my stringer. And trust me: a fish has to be really special to make it onto my stringer. Otherwise, it gets tossed back into the water, so I can fish some more.

A man fishes for two reasons: he's either sport fishing or fishing to eat, which means he's either going to try to catch the biggest fish he can, take a picture of it, admire it with his buddies and toss it back to sea, or he's going to take that fish on home, scale it, fillet it, toss it in some cornmeal, fry it up, and put it on his plate. This, I think, is a great analogy for how men seek out women.

See, men are, by nature, hunters, and women have been put in the position of being the prey. Think about it: it used to be that a man "picked" a wife, a man "asked" a woman to dinner, a man had to get "permission" from a woman's father to have her hand in marriage, and even, in some cases, to date her. We pursued—in fact, we've been taught all our lives that it was not only a good thing to chase women, but natural. Women have bought into this for years, too; how many times have you or one of your girls said, "I like it when a man pursues me," or "I need him to romance me and give me flowers and make me feel like I'm wanted"? Flowers, jewelry, phone calls, dates, sweet talk—these are all the weapons in our hunting arsenal when we're coming for you.

But the question always remains: once we hook you, what will we do with you? Taking a cue from my love of fishing, my philosophy is that men will treat women like one of these two things: a sports fish or a keeper. How we meet, how the conversation goes, how the relationship develops, and the demands you make on a man will all determine whether you'll be treated like a sports fish—a throwback—or a keeper, the kind of woman a man can envision settling down with. And the way we separate the two is very simple, as I explain next.

A SPORTS FISH . . .

Doesn't have any rules, requirements, respect for herself, or guidelines, and we men can pick up her scent a mile away. She's the party girl who takes a sip of her Long Island iced tea or a shot of her Patrón, then announces to her suitor that she just wants to "date and see how it goes," and she's the conservatively dressed woman at the office who is a master at networking, but clueless about how to approach men. She has no plans for any ongoing relationships, is not expecting anything in particular from a man, and sets absolutely not nary one condition or restriction on anyone standing before her—she makes it very clear that she's just along for whatever is getting ready to happen. For sure, as soon as she lets a man know through words and action that he can treat her just any old kind of way, he will do just that. Men will stand in line to sign up for that, believe me.

A KEEPER . . .

Never gives in easily, and the standards/requirements start the moment you open your mouth. See, she understands her power and wields it like a samurai sword. She commands—not demands—respect, just by the way she carries herself. You can walk up to her and give her your best game, and while she may be impressed by what you say, that's no guarantee that she's going to let the conversation go any further, much less give you her phone number and agree to give you some of her valuable time. Men automatically know from the moment she opens her mouth that if they want her, they'll have to get in line with her standards and requirements, or keep it moving because she's done with the games and isn't interested in playing. But she will also send all the signals that she is capable of being loyal to a man and taking good care of him, appreciative of what he's bringing to the relationship, and ready for love—true, long-lasting love.

*N*ewsflash: it's not the guy who determines whether you're a sports fish or a keeper—it's you. (Don't hate the player, hate the game.) When a man approaches you, you're the one with total control over the situation—whether he can talk to you, buy you a drink, dance with you, get your number, take you home, see you again, all of that. We certainly want these things from you; that's why we talked to you in the first place. But it's you who decides if you're going to give us any of the things we want, and how, exactly, we're going to get them. Where you stand in our eyes is dictated by *your* control over the situation. Every word you say, every move you make, every signal you give to a man will help him determine whether he should try to play you, be straight with you, or move on to the next woman to do a little more sport fishing.

I like to think that the way you play this situation is much like how you climb the ladder at work. Think about it: dating is a lot like a business; the best way to become successful is to master and control things you have control over. When I first started in show business, I knew I wanted to be a top-flight comedian. But because the club owners didn't know me well, all I could get was a gig as the opening act—the first guy up, fifteen minutes to do my thing, and then off the stage I went. Still, I knew that if I was on my game—showed up on time, networked, and, most important, gave thought-provoking, funny performances that made the audiences and the club owners remember me—I could get the ultimate job as the headliner, the comedian who gets his name on the marquee and forty-five minutes to make people scream with laughter. I controlled my fifteen minutes by making people laugh hard enough to remember me, and then parlayed it into gigs as the "featured" comedian, the performer who gets thirty minutes on the stage. And then I did the same thing with my thirty minutes onstage, making people laugh so hard that club owners didn't have any other choice but to make me the featured act.

See? My success in getting to be one of the Kings of Comedy was based on my desire and ability to control my product—my performance—which ultimately made me exactly who I wanted to be. And doing that got me exactly what I wanted—success. The same applies to a woman who wants to be a "keeper" rather than a sports fish. You control what you can control—your image, the way you conduct yourself, the way you let men talk to and approach you—and use that to get the relationship you want.

Let me bring it home for you: imagine you're in the health club, and you're on the stair climber, in your tight red athletic bra and matching form-fitting spandex gym pants, glistening and dewy with sweat, getting your workout on, looking really fit and sexy. A good-looking guy comes in—he's handsome, fit, no rings on his fingers. And when he walks up to the treadmill next to where you're working out, the chemistry between the two of you is electric; he smiles, you smile back; you move to another machine, he moves to one not too far from you; he glances at you, you glance back. And when the two of you are finished working out, he goes all out—comes up to you and breaks the ice.

"Looked like you had a good workout," he might say, looking you in your eyes, and then letting his gaze linger somewhere around your hips. "A woman who takes good care of herself. Nice."

How you respond—the way you control this exchange—will mean all the difference between whether he considers you a throwback or a keeper. Say something akin to "You know, a girl's gotta look hot," and then twirl around so he can get a better view, and that man is going to do a mental calculation of just how fast he can get you into the bed, and whether he can suddenly switch his workout time so he doesn't have to see you again after he hits it. A man will determine just from those seven words and that tiny action that you're a woman who can be easily had—someone who's out for a good time and is getting herself in shape solely to keep her body looking right so that guys can look at it and *really* enjoy it. I assure you, the next few sentences out of his mouth likely will involve some serious attempts to reel you in, and, if you bite, he'll get you hook, line, and sinker. And then he'll keep it moving.

But respond to him by saying something like "Thanks, my health is important to me and working out is a great way to keep in shape," and he knows that he's going to have to dig a little deeper to find out more about you. This is no guarantee that he will think you're a keeper—you'll have to do a bit more talking than that simple line—but at the very least, he won't immediately peg you as a throwback. Your comments may lead him to talk about why he works out, which could lead to a meaningful conversation about a mutual interest you both have for staying in shape. And that could lead to him asking more questions, for which a keeper will have plenty of answers—laced, of course, with enough requirements to let this man know that you're a keeper, someone who is looking for a man who will stick around.

Now, revealing that you're a keeper is no guarantee that this guy won't just walk away. Some men really are just sport fishing and have no intention of doing anything more than throwing back the women they bed. If this is the case with this man, then let him walk—what do you care? He's not the guy you're looking for. I know that you and your girls have been told for years on end that you just don't pass up any opportunities when a man walks your way—he could be The One. But I'm here to tell you that this philosophy is just plain dumb. Women are smart—you all can tell when your friends are lying, you know when your kids are up to no good, co-workers can't get anything past you at the job. You're quick to let each one of them know that you're not stupid, that you see them coming a mile away, and you're not going to let them play that game with you. But when it comes to your relationships with the opposite sex, all of that goes out the window; you relinquish your power and lose all control over the situation—cede it to any old man who looks at you twice. Just because he happened to look at you twice.

All I'm telling you to do is be smart about it. Know that if this man isn't looking for a serious relationship, you're not going to change his mind just because you two are going out on dates and being intimate. You could be the most perfect woman on the Lord's green earth—you're capable of interesting conversation, you cook a mean breakfast, you hand out backrubs like sandwiches, you're independent (which means, to him, that you're not going to be in his pockets)—but if he's not ready for a serious relationship, he's going to treat you like a sports fish. A perfect example of this is in this "Strawberry Letter"—these are letters the *Steve Harvey Morning Show* receives from its listeners—sent in by a woman who clearly was just starting to realize she was nothing more than a plaything:

> I have been seeing this man for six months and everything seemed cool until January of this year. We've gone out and visited each other's homes, but all of a sudden, he's stopped calling and when I call him, he seems excited, but then he is very short with me. He plans trips and cancels them. And when I ask him if we should cut off all communication, he says "no." But he doesn't act like he wants to be bothered. I don't know what happened, and I still like him, but it just bothers me to know that something could be on his mind that he is not sharing with me or maybe he has found a woman and wants to keep me in his back pocket.

He's sport fishing, and in her heart, she knows this. But she's still trying to hang in there and see if he's going to do right by her. Any woman in this situation should just leave that guy alone. Instead of investing all this time and energy in a man who can't and won't live up to your expectations, let that guy walk. And then when the next man comes along, take control and let him know your ground rules up front (see my chapter "Men Respect Standards—Get Some"): "I don't take phone calls after 10 P.M., because my kids are asleep and I'm getting my rest"; "I appreciate a man who shows up when he says he's going to show up and calls when he's going to be late"; and "I don't have sex with anyone until I'm sure that we are in a serious, committed relationship—no casual sex for me" are all acceptable ground rules for any man coming at you. If those ground rules are too much for him, he's going to walk away because he's sport fishing.

If, however, he has something going for himself, and he knows that in order to complete his life he needs a woman who has something going for herself, he's going to stick around and keep the conversation going. That's the man who is willing to put in work—who knows that he's not going to just romance you, get what he wants, and walk away. That guy right there? He's your man. He's fishing for a keeper, and after he's proven himself worthy of your time, then you can let him take you on home, fillet you, put some cornmeal on you, fry you up, and serve you up on a delicious plate.

Need more examples of differences between sports fish and keepers? Read on:

1. A woman who commands respect is a keeper; a woman who lets men get away with disrespecting her is a throwback.

2. A woman who is dressed appropriately—has her goodies reasonably covered, but is still sexy, is a keeper; a woman who is scantily clad and dripping sex is a throwback.

3. A woman who won't let you feel all over her body while you're dancing is a keeper; a woman who drops it like it's hot and puts on a dance floor performance that would make video vixen Karrine Steffans blush is a throwback.

4. A woman who takes a man's number but doesn't give him her own is a keeper; a woman who hands out her home, work, and cell phone numbers and e-mail and home addresses to a man who's done nothing more than buy her a drink and ask how he can reach her is a throwback.

5. A woman who can hold a respectful, respectable conversation with a man and his mother is a keeper; a woman who shudders at the prospect of having to talk to the matriarch of a man's family is a throwback.

6. A woman who can adapt to any situation thrown at her—she can hold her own at the PTA meeting, in the boardroom, in a restaurant, at a sporting event— is a keeper; a woman who can't put together a coherent sentence or makes it clear she has no interest in doing so is a throwback.

7. A woman who knows she wants to be married and raise a family and lets a man know this up front is a keeper; a woman who doesn't have a plan for her relationship life beyond next weekend is a throwback.

8. A woman whom we can introduce to our friends and family is a keeper; a woman we don't even bother introducing to our friends or family is a throwback.

9. A woman who smiles and takes care of herself and is generally happy with her life is a keeper; a woman who doesn't take care of herself and is sour all the time, has an attitude wider than all the ocean, and

doesn't hesitate to lay somebody out for the slightest transgression is a throwback.

10. A woman who shows her appreciation for all that you do for her is a keeper; a woman who acts like nothing you do can make her happy is a throwback.

11. A woman who is loyal is a keeper; a woman who always has her eye out for the next best thing is a throwback.

12. A woman who understands that a man validates his manhood by who he is, what he does, and how much he makes, and who knows how to finesse her relationship so that her man feels like he's handling his business is a keeper; a woman who wields her paycheck and influence like a sword and belittles his career and financial contributions is a throwback.

How to tell if you've met someone looking for a keeper or a throwback:

1. If his conversation with you is extremely superficial, and never seems to graduate beyond the surface, he's sport fishing; if he genuinely seems interested in your

needs, life, desires, and future, then he's looking for a keeper.

2. If he laughs off your requirements and standards, then he's sport fishing; if he seems willing to abide by your rules, and actually follows through on them, then he's looking for a keeper.

3. If he takes your phone number but waits longer than twenty-four hours to call, he's sport fishing; if he calls you right away, he's showing that he's genuinely interested in you, and is most likely looking for a keeper.

4. If he takes you out on a date and lets you pay, or only kicks in his portion of the bill, he's sport fishing; if he pays the bill, he's showing that he's willing to provide for you, which means he's likely looking for a keeper.

5. If he tells you he's going to be somewhere at a certain time, and he consistently shows up late without so much as the courtesy of a phone call, he's probably sport fishing; if he shows up when he's supposed to, he's looking for a keeper.

6. If you never meet his friends, family, co-workers, or other people who are important to him, he's sport

fishing; if he introduces you to his people, he might be looking for a keeper.

7. If he keeps offering up excuses for why he can't meet your friends and family, he's sport fishing; if he agrees to go to the family barbecue or a social event where he will be introduced to family, friends, and co-workers, he might consider you a keeper.

8. If he cringes at the mere mention of children, he's sport fishing; if he's willing to meet your kids and shows up with gifts and can relate to them in a way that makes them comfortable with him, then he might consider you and your kids keepers.

9. If he does not have himself together financially, emotionally, and spiritually, he may be sport fishing; if he is capable of providing and protecting his potential family the way a real man should, then he might be searching for a keeper.

10. If he lobbies for an "open" relationship and says he's cool with you seeing other people, then he's sport fishing; if he wants your relationship to be exclusive and he agrees to date only you, he considers you a keeper.

7

MAMA'S BOYS

Every day on the *Steve Harvey Morning Show,* my cohost Shirley and I have a really popular segment called "Strawberry Letter 23," during which we invite our listeners to let us help them solve their problems. We get all kinds of e-mails and letters from people desperate for advice on how to handle wild kids, overly demanding bosses, cheating boyfriends, out-of-control baby's mommas, money-grubbing family members, horrible friendships—you name it, we hear about it. Some of the questions are extremely sad, some of them are so surprising they make you want to clutch your chest, and some of them just make you shake your head and wonder how the person asking for advice made it through. The people who write those letters aren't doing it in a vacuum; for every problem addressed in "Strawberry Letter 23," there are thousands of listeners out there dealing with the same drama in their own lives. We give our opinions on the situation, and some sound suggestions for how they can get out of the mess they're in with the hope that the advice we're passing on helps not only the person who wrote us, but the legions of fans also looking for answers.

A lot of the "Strawberry Letters" touch me, but one that stood out to me recently was from a woman who wrote an attention getter in the subject line: Did I Marry a Man or a Boy? She went on to say that she's a thirty-five-year-old woman who is married to a thirty-year-old man she'd dated for ten years before they got married about six months ago. She claimed that although their relationship is great, his "controlling" mother is driving her crazy. Here's some of what she wrote:

> She controls my husband like he is a little child. She calls on him to do everything. She calls my house late at night and I can hear her through the phone, screaming at him about something that she may not have agreed on. She calls on him for money, to paint her house, to pick her up from the movies, to cook for special occasions, and even wash her clothes. What prompted me to write this letter is the fact that it is now 10:42 P.M., and I am home alone because my husband was just called by his mother to come to her house to help bake cakes for a fund-raiser tomorrow. I had plans to spend

time with my husband tonight, but once again, his mother got in the way. Don't get me wrong: I love the fact that he respects and helps his mother, but sometimes I feel left out. My kids and I are often put on the back burner because he is always doing something for his mother. All these years I have kept my thoughts about this to myself, but I don't know how much more I can take . . . his mother is always taking away from our family. I sometimes feel like I didn't marry a man . . . I need him to be a man and take control.

Now I sympathize for "Did I Marry a Man or a Boy?" I hear from all too many women who face the same problem: their men are excessively attached to their mothers at an age where you expect the sons to be totally independent—it's a bond that allows the mothers of these men to exert all kinds of control over their lives, usually to the detriment of romantic relationships. The mother says, "Jump," the son asks, "How high and when do you need me to be back?" and the girlfriend/wife rolls her eyes and sits in the corner with her mouth poked out, wondering (a) why this grown man just can't fix his mouth to say no every once in a while, (b) why this woman holds so much power over her man, and (c) what kind of tool can she buy/rent/borrow/invent to detach the two of them so that she and her man can get back to the business of building a life together. No matter what they say, no matter what they do, no matter how many different ways they slice it, women like "Did I Marry a Man or a Boy?" feel like they just can't compete with The Other Woman—the mother. Those same women will toss up more motives than a DA to explain why their man proudly answers to the mama's boy title: his mother refuses to cut the umbilical cord and let him be a man; his mother doesn't think there's a woman alive good enough for him; his mother has something against his significant other; he doesn't want to grow up; he jumps through hoops for his mother because she spoils him rotten and takes care of his every need. We've heard them all.

To "Did I Marry a Man or a Boy?" and all the other women in relationships with mama's boys, I say: stop coming up with excuses, and recognize that he's a mama's boy because you let him be one.

Yes, I said it: It's. Your. Fault.

Let me tell you why a man will get up out of a warm bed with a beautiful naked woman in it, pull on his clothes, grab his keys, and get in his car at 10:42 P.M., with his children and woman in the house alone, to drive all the way across town to bake cakes doggone near the middle of the night for his mother's bake sale: because his mother has set requirements and standards for that man, and his woman has not.

Look, I already told you how this works: a man who loves you will be the man you need him to be if you have requirements—standards you set to make the relationship work the way you want it to. A real man is happy and eager to live by your rules, as long as he knows what the rules are and he's sure that abiding by those rules will help keep the woman he loves happy. The only thing you have to do is establish the rules, say them out loud early in the relationship, and make sure he sticks to them.

But if you don't have any standards or requirements, guess whose rules he's going to follow? That's right, his mother's. She was the first woman to tell him what she would and would not accept; if she told him to wash his hands before he sat at the dinner table, be back in the house before the streetlights came on, go to Sunday school on Sundays, protect his sister when the two of them were out, and always—always—listen to and trust his mother, guess what this boy was going to do? He was going to follow those rules to the letter (mostly), because he did not want to deal with the consequences that came if he didn't listen to and respect his mother. He also followed those rules because he loved his mother, and her rules (mostly) never changed; oh, they adapted to his age and circumstances, but a mother always keeps some rules front and center for the men in her life, no matter her son's station in life, including respecting her, loving her unconditionally, and protecting and providing for the woman who gave him life. She never relinquishes those standards and requirements, and her son, if he's a responsible, thoughtful, loving son, doesn't really ever break away from them.

Until, that is, he finds a woman he loves and who loves him back and has sense enough to set some ground rules and requirements for the relationship, chief among them the following:

1. You need to respect me.

2. You must put me and our kids after God and above all others.

3. Be clear to everyone involved in our lives that they will respect your relationship—and me.

Now, if you've never set those rules up, and his mother's never relinquished hers, is it a wonder that he's going to leave you in the bed naked while he goes to bake cakes? It's not that she has a hold on this man; it's that you never bothered to take the reins. Think about what "Did I Marry a Man or a Boy?" said: she's been in a relationship with her husband for ten and a half years, and not once did she step forward and express her displeasure when her man's mother called the house to put him to work. "All these years I have kept my thoughts about this to myself . . ." she wrote. So if she never told her man she doesn't like it when he leaves her and the kids to run over to his mother's house, and she doesn't like it when he allows his mother to yell at him like a child, and she doesn't want him cooking, painting, driving, and doing laundry for his mother when she needs him to do things around their house, how, exactly, was he supposed to know that his interactions with his mother violate his wife's standards? Men cannot read minds, and we are completely incapable of anticipating what you want.

So you have to speak up.

She didn't say it in the letter, but my guess is that "Did I Marry a Man or a Boy?" failed to speak up about her mother-in-law's abuse of power for over a decade because she was afraid that he would leave her—that if she tried to drive a wedge between her man and his mom, he'd choose his mother over her. I'll tell you, though, that men don't work this way; if your man truly loves you and he's a real man, he'll figure out a way to get his mom onboard with making his woman happy—to smooth everything out so that the relationship can work for all parties involved.

First, acknowledge that you can't compete with this woman: she changed his diapers, she can cook his favorite dish exactly the way he likes it, she knows most of—if not all—of his friends, and she's known him longer than anybody. Her blood courses through his veins. If he loves his mother and they have a good relationship, you're not going to get in the middle of that. (And honestly, you'll realize it's much better to be in a relationship with a man who loves his mother than it is to be with someone who can't stand the woman who gave birth to him; I'm going to go out on a limb here and say that the latter probably won't ever be able to commit to a loving, stable relationship with a woman if he couldn't get that single most important, obvious, easy male/female relationship right, but the guy who loves his mother and treats her with respect is the guy who will know how to act with you.) But you most certainly can work with your man and his mom by controlling what you do have control over—by using your powers to set standards and requirements that he needs to abide by as the two of you work to create a family or to blend your families together. Instead of writing an angry "Strawberry Letter" in the middle of the night when her man tiptoed out of the house to help his mom, "Did I Marry a Man or a Boy?" should have stopped her husband at the bedroom door and told him something like, "Look, I know you love your mother and you'd do anything for her, but it's not acceptable to me for you to leave me and these babies here in this house alone to bake cookies. If you choose to go over there, then you need to stay over there for the night."

This would not have been evil or unreasonable. Leaving a woman and children in the house at a quarter to eleven at night—whether to bake cookies or go to the strip club—is unacceptable if that woman thinks it is. And if she lets her man know this, she's making him aware of the standards he needs to live up to in order to stay in their relationship. Once it's said, the ball is in his court. He can either go bake cookies, or he can be a man and call his mother and set it straight—tell her he can't come by tonight, but he can drop off some store-bought baked goods in the morning before he leaves for work. His mother may not be happy about this, but what would you care? Again, you can't control how she feels about her son's actions, and you can't control her son's actions, but you can control how you feel and what you expect of your man.

Now, "Did I Marry a Man or a Boy?" waited almost eleven years to have her say, but if you're just now getting into a relationship with a man, you're going to have to get this thing out on the table. Tell him that you don't ever want to come between him and his mother, but you sure don't want to compete with her, either, so he'll have to do what he has to do to let his mother know that (a) under no certain terms are the needs of his girlfriend/fiancée/wife ever going to come second, and (b) she should respect his need to be a protector and provider for the woman to whom he's professed his love. Don't worry, he understands his need to do this; no real man anywhere needs his mother more than he needs his woman. He recognizes pretty early on that the support he gets from his mother—clothes, housing, education, nurturing, and so on—needs to come to an end when manhood is full throttle, and that if he is to have a true, loving, lasting relationship with a woman, he needs to cut the proverbial umbilical cord from his mom so that he can give life to his new family—his own family.

All you have to do is speak up.

Tell him straight up: "I need you here to protect and provide for us, to give us security in our lives, to help raise these children, to set an example for this boy, who needs to see what real men do, and for this girl, who needs to know what a real man is so she can find one of her own someday. I need you to be the head of this family."

Lay it out like this, and your requirements will trump his mother's every time.

8

WHY MEN CHEAT

From the male perspective, the answers to the question "Why do men cheat?" are crystal clear. Not so much for women. No matter how good or sensible the reasons are, men know that women will never hear one and say, "Oh! Now I get it!" There are neither words big enough nor experts with enough credentials and letters behind their name to slice it and dice it up in a way that's palatable for most women; inevitably, responses to this million-dollar question are always going to sound like ten-dollar answers.

And who could argue with that? For (most) women, after all, cheating is unthinkable and (at first blush) unforgivable—you don't and can't comprehend why a man would be unfaithful, and you won't ever pretend to. You figure that if you've told him you love him; given him your mind, your body, and your time;

moved in with him; shared the bills with him; done his laundry; cooked his food; borne his children; and said an enthusiastic, "I do," in front of the Lord, the pastor, your mother, and all her best friends and yours, too, the least your man can do is honor what is most sacred to you: the promise of fidelity. He can lie (every once in a while), fall down on the housework and the child rearing, get a little lax in the income department, pay more attention to his boys and his mother than he does to you, and slip into the mediocre category when it comes to the boudoir—even say the Lord's name in vain while you're walking out the door to go to yet another church service alone.

But let a man step out on his woman, and watch the earth move.

That's my way of saying that women will put up with a lot of things.

Cheating is not one of them.

Now, we men? We understand this. We know what it takes to tip, we're capable of calculating the collateral damage that comes with getting caught, and we know that getting back into the graces of the woman we cheated on—and her mother, and her friends, and anyone else who's sympathized with her having to resurrect herself from such a devastating life event—will require a Herculean effort.

Still, we do it.

Why?

I am not here to justify a cheating man's actions. Rather, this is my humble attempt to explain to you why a man might go on ahead and get a little something on the side, and what you can do to cut down the chances that your man will do this to you. So let's just go on ahead and get right to it. Men cheat because. . .

They can.

Dress it up any way you want to, but men don't view sex the way you women do, plain and simple. For a lot of you, the act of intercourse is emotional—an act of love. That's understandable, considering the sheer physics of the act; you have to lie back and allow a foreign object to enter your body. You've been taught all your life that you only let that kind of deeply intimate moment happen with someone who really means something to you.

By contrast, when it comes to men and sex, neither emotions nor meaning necessarily enter the equation. It's easy—very easy—for a man to have sex, go home, wash it off with soap and water, and act like what he just did never happened. Sex can be a purely physical act for us—love has absolutely nothing to do with it. Consider this "Strawberry Letter" from a woman who called herself "Concerned":

> During a conversation with my husband of 20 years, I asked him if he would honestly always be satisfied with having sex with me only. He hesitated for so long before answering

that I just knew he was going to say "no." He then went on to explain that he loved me and would never do anything to hurt me, but if I gave him permission to have sex with other women and not form relationships with them, he would. He said that as he's gotten older, he's been wondering if he is still attractive and sexually appealing, and that attention from another younger woman would boost his ego. Then he asked me if I would be willing to give him permission to have sex with other women if he promised to let them know up front that it's only sex he's interested in and he's not interested in a relationship. He even offered to answer any questions I'd have with his encounters, or, if I didn't want to know about it, to just do it and not tell me what and when it happened. Obviously, he's got a problem with monogamy. Should I consent so that a potential for sneaking around can be eliminated? What can I do to get him to change his thinking—if anything?

The answer to that last question in the "Strawberry Letter" is, not much. A man can love his wife, his children, his home, and the life that they've all built together, and have an incredible physical connection to her, and *still* get some from another woman without a second thought about it, because the actual act with the other woman meant nothing to him. It was something that may have made him feel good physically, but emotionally, his heart—the professing, providing, and protecting he saves for the woman he loves—may be at home with his woman.

Now filter that bit of information through the lens of, say, a high-powered man who has a wife whose job is equally prestigious and demanding. I don't profess to know what goes on behind closed doors in that kind of household, but by all public accounts, that couple could be perfectly happy, in love, supportive—down for each other. Still, her job could take her overseas, leaving her man at home to run the household, take care of the kids, and keep up his demanding work schedule for weeks on end, without so much as a hot-and-heavy phone conversation to help him make it through the enormous time period he'd have to go without having sex. Trust me when I say this: under this situation, plenty of men would easily justify their getting some from somewhere else. Neither he, nor any other man, for that matter, is going to go without sex too long. It's not that he doesn't love his wife. But he's there, coming home exhausted from a hard day's work, cooking dinner, shuttling the kids around to all their after-school functions, and checking homework. He's stressed out, and plenty of us men can hear what he may have worked out in his mind: I'm going to go over here and let this other woman tighten me up, and then I'll come back and cook, shuttle, and work until the woman I love comes back to me.

This may seem like a cold piece of work to you, but to a man, it's reasonable. He's got to try to feel better some kind of way, and so he's going to get sex from someone if he can't get it from you. You see it as betrayal. Men see it as just a way to get tightened up, especially if. . .

They think they can get away with it.

Of course, men will consider the risks of getting caught cheating on his lady. But mostly, men initiate affairs pretty confident that they're going to get away with it, and most certainly with all kinds of confidence that if they get caught, their denials will see them through. I used to do a joke where I would encourage men to ride their lie all the way out. I told them, "I don't care if somebody got a picture of my butt up in the air in the pump position with my social security number stamped on the left-hand side of my cheek, I'm going to tell my wife, 'It ain't me—I don't know who that is with my social security number all over his butt, with the same shoes as me, but that's not me!'"

Now, that's my joke, but most men don't consider getting caught a laughing matter. A man who cheats has most certainly calculated the collateral damage that would come from getting busted—potential loss of the woman he loves, his children, his home, and his peace of mind—and he recognizes that this would be a devastating blow to all the things that matter in his life. We all are quite familiar with the saying "Hell hath no fury like a woman scorned," and men understand its meaning much better than you do; we know the hell is coming and there will be plenty of scorn if we get busted.

Still, men don't really ever think they're going to get caught. Basically, we think we're slick and we go to great lengths to hide our infidelity from you, always with this in mind: if you don't know about it, it can't hurt you. We're pretty confident that your willingness to be in a relationship with us supersedes all the things we do that look suspicious, because we know you'll work through the suspicion—that it's more important to you to be with us in our imperfection than to leave us and be alone. At least that's what we're hoping. And in the beginning, mostly, you will. But the moment your suspicions turn into a *Law & Order*–type investigation, we're going to lie and deny.

That's if we care about you.

But if not—if a man doesn't see you fitting into his life plan—he won't even bother with all of the covering up and the chitchat after he gets found out. He'll simply tell you that he was sleeping with someone else because. . .

He hasn't become who he wants and needs to be or found who he truly wants.

You may think this is a cop-out, but it is the reality. It goes back to the way men judge themselves against each other: I told you in the introduction and have reiterated elsewhere in the book that we are defined by who we are, what we do, and how much we make. And if we haven't gotten to where we want and need to be, then we're not going to be ready to figure out how settling down with one woman fits into our plans for becoming a truly independent, mature, well-off man. I mean, how many times have you seen or been in a relationship where the man says over and over again, "When I get my money right, I'll think about commitment," or, "I just need to get that promotion first, then I'll settle down." That guy is still trying to complete himself, and while he's working toward that, he's not organizing his life to include a committed relationship. He tells himself he simply doesn't have time for it—it's simply not a priority for him. And so creep he will.

The same can be true, even, of a man who is married with children. The man who is mature and has figured out who he is and is happy with what he does and how much he makes probably has his life ordered up correctly; he's become the man he envisioned himself being and has put his priorities in this order: God, family, education, business, and then everything else. But if family isn't second, it's about to be a problem; he's going to dedicate himself to whatever his priorities are, in the order in which he's put them. Even if he's already said, "I do," and held his babies in his arms and done everything a man's supposed to do to protect and provide for them, if he's decided that it's more important to him to fulfill that hunting jones, then that's going to be the priority for him—he's not going to sync up with your demand that he be faithful. He's not going to rub it in your face, and he's going to do everything he can to preserve what he has with you, but he's still going to have a little something on the side. Really, it's got nothing to do with you.

I have a friend who's successful, has plenty of money, a beautiful family—the ideal life. And one evening while we were sitting around with a few of our friends shooting the breeze about how satisfied we are with our stations in life, my boy announced with a slick grin, "I love my wife, man, but I got this cold one on the side." We were surprised—don't get me wrong. But we accepted that from him because we all know that this man hasn't got his priorities right yet, and there's nothing we can do or say to make him do it. He knows that once he's stepped out on his wife, he's putting something else before God and family. But only he can put his house in order. Now, if he's young, that might come with mental maturity; the old-timers say all the time that experience is priceless—too bad you have to pay for it with your youth. Of course, maturity and age go hand in hand, but circumstances bring it about, too: if a man is a spiritual person and he's got a relationship with God, he'll mature much more quickly, just because his beliefs will hold him to a much more stringent moral code. And that moral code will automatically make him put family second, because this is what a relationship with God demands. Now, he'll make it a priority to find a woman who completes his life, someone who can be the mother of his children—who can make his unit complete.

Sometimes men wise up without God in their lives. I have a buddy who had all kinds of women doing all kinds of things to him and for him, and he finally got into a position where he said, "Man, I got all these women and I can get them to do all these things and give me all these things, but I'm not happy. I don't have any peace and I just don't feel like I have my life together." And right then and there, he made the decision to stop treating women the way he'd been treating them and get what he was finally yearning for: a family. His philandering stopped cold. He's not saved. He didn't have some big revelation with God, he didn't get called to the ministry. He just decided he needed to do something different to find the joy in his life, and the only way he could find that was with someone, and only one someone, special.

When a man finds that joy—the chances of his cheating get really slim. Unless. . .

What's happening at home isn't "happening" like it used to.

That's right, I said it: it could have something to do with you. Your man may be walking around telling himself that your relationship just doesn't have that spark anymore, that you don't turn him on like you used to—that you don't come on to him like you did when the two of you first fell in love. You know how it goes: the two of you get comfortable with each other, settle in, have some babies, buy a house, and then get bogged down in the bills and raising the kids and going to work and keeping up with the rat race that comes when you're a family trying to make it. The next thing he knows, the woman who used to wear and do little things to keep it hot and spicy isn't interested in doing that little thing she did when the two of them first got together. In fact, the sex has become uninspired; she's coming in from work, where she was dressed up in her nice skirt and heels and makeup and such, and she's breaking down before she can get to the door good. And now, after a long day at work, and even more work when she gets home, she's coming to bed in a head scarf and a T-shirt and is this close to hiring a firing squad to take you out for even looking at her with those bedroom eyes.

In other words, what's back at the house has become ho-hum—routine. And this man is missing the spark that used to be there. You've changed. (He knows he's changed, too, but we're not talking about him, we're talking about you.) Perhaps that comes, too, with a feeling that you don't appreciate him like you used to. The thank-yous come less frequently, there's a lot of arguing going on—turmoil seems to get up with you in the morning and cuddle up with the two of you at night. And your home just isn't feeling like what he signed up for. And if he can't get what he signed up for back at the house, he's more likely to go out and find it somewhere else, because guess what? He knows he can always go find it somewhere else, particularly since. . .

The Biggest Reason of All: There's always a woman out there willing to cheat with him.

That's the truth that no woman wants to face. Imagine if every woman said, "You're married—I can't do that with you." Man, do you know how many marriages and relationships would still exist today? Men *can* cheat because there are so many women willing to give themselves to a man who doesn't belong to them. Sure, every now and again there are women who get fooled and don't know that a man is already spoken for. A majority of the time, however, these women know they're sleeping with a married man. Yes, these are the women who have no standards and requirements and who suffer from serious self-esteem issues, making themselves willing to cheat and available to be cheated on. If those women took themselves out of the cheater's circle, the incidence of cheating would be cut seriously down. And the way to get out of that cheater's circle is to do exactly what I'm teaching you to do in this book: figure out your standards and requirements, explain them, and stick to them (Chapter 9), get to *really* know the man by asking five essential questions you'll need to know to move a relationship forward (see Chapter 10), and follow the Ninety-Day Rule (see Chapter 11). And then teach all of this to your daughters, too. If we don't, after all, break that cycle, the cheating will continue.

So, ladies, the reasons I've given here are the primary reasons men cheat, but trust me, there are many, many more. A man is always going to have a reason to justify why he's doing wrong, and those reasons will change from man to man and woman to woman. What's important for you to understand, though, is that regardless of a man's reasons, he knows what you know: it's wrong to commit to someone and promise to remain faithful and then go against that—especially if this was one of your mate's requirements. Women can go over it again and again in their minds, finding all kinds of deficiencies in themselves—"I didn't do this right," "I wasn't good enough," "I didn't love him the way I should," "she came in here and outperformed me"—but the fact still remains that he didn't have any business cheating. So women need to release themselves from the blame of a cheating man's actions—just do that for yourselves. Because holding on to that baggage can be paralyzing; it can cripple you and keep you from performing in your next encounter. You simply cannot drive forward if you're focused on what's happening in the rearview mirror.

You can, however, limit the amount of times you're cheated on again. You do that by upping the ante on your requirements. See, you have a lot more power to limit the things that happen to you—you've got the power of persuasion, your power of intuition, your power of suggestion, standards to help keep you protected. If you let a man know up front that you'll tolerate a lot of things but cheating is not one of them, then he's really clear on the fact that if he steps out of the union, he stays out of the union. And if he breaks that promise and steps out anyway? You've got to be prepared to let him go and walk away. You can't find out your man cheated, confront him about it, and then stay with him, only to question his every move and nag him about what he's doing every chance you get. Because that simply means you never really forgave him, and you're creating a situation that's ripe for him to cheat again. You've got to either let him go, or find it in your heart to truly forgive the man and work on a way to move forward with him.

Now sometimes, it takes a man to lose something or nearly lose something to really appreciate it. But isn't that true of everybody? Some men cheat because there's never been a penalty for it. But if a man who's cheated on you sees you walking out the door and you matter to him, please know that at this point he's very vulnerable and open to learning. Should he win you back, he's going to straighten up and fly right because he's almost lost his girl and his family, which means he'll do most anything you tell him to get back into your good graces. He's going to work to earn your trust back—follow your requirements to get back on the team. If that means he has to be home by a certain time, call when he's going to be late, send flowers every week, find a sitter so you all can have a date night on Thursdays, go to church with you on Sundays, even sit on a psychologist's couch and air out all of your dirty laundry until you're satisfied he's a changed man, then that's what he'll do.

Once there's a penalty and he's forced to say to himself, "Wow, everything I've ever loved was about to be lost," he may very well come through the fire a better man.

Is that to say it's going to be easy to forgive him and not be suspicious? No. But he may eventually earn your trust back and be willing to work through it with you. He's not going to like being asked questions about where he's been, he's going to hate not being able to be intimate with you while you work through your anger, and he's going to be really reluctant to carry his butt down to the psychologist's office with you. But in his heart of hearts, he knows that's a part of working his way back into your heart. He knows he created this—he knows what he did, and he understands the consequences, ramifications, and repercussions way better than you think he does. We understand penalties, and we know it's going to be straight hell. Trust me, I know. Because it's happened to me. It happens to a lot of men. You can't be a man of power and not step outside your house. I don't know one man of power who has not stepped outside his house. Such a man may exist but I have not met him. But I do know men of power who have learned to do right, go home, and take care of their families. Each one of them eventually gets to that. I certainly have; now, I carry my behind home. I had to come to this, though. And guess what? I know a lot of those same men—entertainers, ball players, executives, and so on—who have turned into some of the best husbands and fathers in the world, because they've lined up their life responsibilities in the right order: God, family, education, and then business. And their wives? They've become better wives in the process, too—by trying to create a little bit of that magic they had when their relationship was fresh and new. She might come home from work and instead of kicking off those heels, keep them on and whisper in his ear to meet her in the bedroom for a pre-dinner snack. Or she might smile a little more, act a little bit more happy, be a tad bit more spontaneous—appreciate her man more, and show it, too.

This was certainly the story of one of my really good friends. His wife found out about his woman on the side, and she left him—went to her mother's house for seven months and took his son with her. Dude was miserable. I mean, he was losing weight. We would go by to get him and say, "Let's go out and have a good time," and he would tell us, "Eh, I don't feel like it." We even offered to take him to see the woman he had on the side, in hopes that at least getting some from her would make him feel a little bit better, but he refused her, too. "I'm through with that," he insisted. "I lost my marriage, my boy is gone—the people who mattered most to me are gone. And I want them back."

It took him a year and a half to get this woman back. I don't know what's going on behind their closed doors, but I'll tell you one thing: she's got the ideal husband now. Any married man can look at him and see how to get it done. But two things had to happen to him: first, he had to find out what was important to him, and what it was like to lose it. And second, he had to come to the realization that he needed to restructure his priorities: God first, then family. And you know what? He goes home every night. He's making money, he's extremely happy, and their family has nothing to worry about. And I heard his wife say, "My new man is something else."

They've been living in their happily ever after for thirty-three years now. He's a helluva dude, man—and she's a lucky lady.

PART THREE

The Playbook

———

How to Win the Game

9

MEN RESPECT STANDARDS—
GET SOME

There are a few things you should know about my wife, Marjorie: She is incredibly talented and supportive. She is just as beautiful on the inside as she is on the outside. She loves the Lord. She is a terrific mother to our children. She's classy and smart. And she cares for, respects, and adores me deeply.

You should also know that my wife has a set of standards that I have known about and respected from the first day I met her.

It started while I was doing a show in Memphis. She walked in with another attractive woman. I couldn't help myself; I stopped mid-joke and said, "Excuse me, I know you don't know me, but one of these days, I'm going to marry you." She laughed and said, "You don't know me." But I didn't care and I told her as much. I knew right then and there we were going to be married some day (of course, this was really more of a hope than a certainty—smile).

Maybe she knew it, too, or at least liked what she saw because even though she disappeared the night I informed her of my plan, she showed up two nights later at another show of mine, and this time, I asked her to come backstage and talk for a while. She agreed, and we became fast friends, and even dated for a spell. But eventually, we both went our separate ways. Still, Marjorie and I always remembered the friendship we had together, and we reached out to check up on each other from time to time.

Finally, Marjorie and I reconnected and started dating again; we got serious pretty quickly, both of us realizing that we had missed out on a great relationship once, and we didn't want to risk losing out on it again. But, even though I knew I was in love with this woman and that she loved me, I was still connected to some women friends I had developed after my divorce, when I had really started dating again.

Well, one particular night when Marjorie was visiting me at my home in New York on Valentine's Day weekend, one of those friends called my cell. I didn't talk much—said, "Hi," told her we'd chat another time and that I'd stop and see her if and when I was back in town, and then hung up. I didn't even think Marjorie heard the conversation—at least she wasn't acting like she did. I should have known better, though. She's got that "mother" hearing—doesn't miss a thing. And sure enough, late that night, when I got up to go to the bathroom—it was about 3:00 A.M.—there was Marjorie in the hallway, standing there in her fur coat with her suitcase in her hand. She was going to leave me—leave us.

"Where you going?" I asked her. Her response made me realize right then and there, in the middle of that hallway, in the middle of the night, that she was The One.

"I'm not trying to be anybody's plaything or anybody's woman on a string," she said matter-of-factly, her suitcase still in her hand. "I don't think you're ready for what I have to offer. I got these kids, I have a good life, and I want a man who will come in and complete my family. If this is what you want, too, I'll be in Memphis."

After I picked up my jaw, I asked her to give me one more chance, took her bags, and immediately found my phone and snapped it in half. I'd lost her once—this beautiful, smart, sweet woman—and no other woman could be as loving and dedicated to me, to us, or to my children. I realized right then and there, in that hallway, that I wanted no other.

In other words, I became the man she needed me to be because she had sense enough to have requirements—standards that she needed in her relationship in order to make the relationship work for her. She knew she wanted a monogamous relationship—a partnership with a man who wanted to be a dedicated husband and father. She also knew this man had to be faithful, love God, and be willing to do what it took to keep this family together. On a smaller scale, she also made clear that she expected to be treated like a lady at every turn—I'm talking opening car doors for her, pulling out her seat when she's ready to sit at the table, coming correct on anniversary, Mother's Day, and birthday gifts, keeping the foul talk to a minimum. These requirements are important to her because they govern how she will be treated; they are important to me, too, because they lay out a virtual map of what all I need to do to make sure she gets what she needs and wants. After all, it's universal knowledge that when mama is happy, everybody is happy. And it is my sole mission in life to make sure Marjorie is happy.

Men can't accomplish this mission for you without your help; we can't possibly begin to fathom what it is you women need and want because your needs and wants change from woman to woman like the wind does from city to city. Men are very simple, logical people; if you tell us what you like and what you don't like, we'll do anything we can to make sure we live up to your expectations, particularly if we're interested in forging a relationship with you. (But beware of telling a man everything you like when you first meet; I'll tell you why later in the chapter.)

But really, we're not programmed to figure it out. It really makes us quite happy when you lay out your requirements for us. And we need you to do it up front, so we can decide if we're up for the challenge—not two weeks into the relationship, not two months after we've had sex, not two years after we've said "I do" in front of the preacher and our respective families and friends. Heck, we'll take them while you're standing there at the bar, sipping on the peach martini we just bought you, so long as you're laying them out. Because now you've given us a road map for how to conduct ourselves, especially if we're truly interested in a relationship with you.

Understand that this chapter is not a license for you to start running down your list of "I can'ts" and "I won'ts" and "you better not nevahs" as soon as a gentleman approaches you. We do like some kind of decorum. You've got to finesse the situation—tell a man what you require without making it feel like you're ticking off a list of demands. It really is all in the delivery; if you tell him your requirements in the midst of conversation, and they sound attainable, and you shape your standards in soft language, it'll be easier for him to understand, and, more important, act on them. Think about how crazy he's going to look at you if, finger wagging, you just come out your face and say, "I will not tolerate a man who does not understand my role as a mother—if you got a problem with my kids and the rest of my family, you got a problem with me!" It'll be the equivalent of the needle scratching all the way across the record; he's going to think, at best, that you're angry—at worst, you're crazy, and perhaps your family is, too. But imagine how he'll feel if you flip the script and say something pleasant like, "Oh, you know,

I have kids and they're number one in my life because my parents raised me to understand the importance of family." Now, he knows you're one of those good girls—sweet, responsible, and family oriented. If he's not that guy, he'll move on to the next woman—the one with no requirements who's down for whatever. But if he's a man who shares your belief in the importance of family, he's going to keep talking to you, and listen for more of your standards.

Here are a few more examples I've laid out for you so you can see how to wrap up your requirements in one of those pretty bows.

***Instead of saying* you "can't stand it" when a man shows up late,** say something like, "Everybody is so busy these days—time sure is precious, isn't it? I go out of my way to make sure that if I say I'm going to be somewhere at 7:00 P.M., I'm going to be there at 7:00 P.M., if not earlier, so that we can do what we need to do in a timely manner, and if I'm going to be late, it only takes a phone call to be courteous."

Translation: You've just told him that you require the man in your life to show up when he says he's going to show up, and have enough manners and class to call if he's going to be late. Now he knows to leave a few minutes earlier so he gets to you on time, and to make sure his cell is charged in case he needs to give you a head's-up.

Instead of saying, **"If you're dating and sleeping with other women, I am not the one!"** say something like, "I'm always honest with the man I'm dating; if I feel like I want to see other people besides him, I let him know up front so that he can decide if he wants to continue the relationship as is, or ask me to date him exclusively."

Translation: You've just told him that you require the man in your life to be honest and up front about the parameters of the relationship—if he's going to play, he's going to have to let you know so that you can make intelligent, rational decisions about how to deal with that. You've told him, too, that this is up for discussion—that the two of you can decide together what it is you want out of the relationship, instead of having it dictated to him.

Instead of saying, **"If my man doesn't have God in his life and doesn't know how to jog for Jesus, there's no need in him even opening his mouth to me,"** perhaps you can say something like, "Sunday is my favorite day of the week, because I get to go to church and fellowship with like-minded people and exercise my faith. By the time service is over, I feel so uplifted, I know the rest of my week is going to go great."

Translation: You've made clear that you're a God-fearing, churchgoing woman who knows the Lord and takes her faith seriously, and you've opened up the conversation for him to give his take on how he feels about religion and spirituality.

Instead of saying, **"I got three kids and two jobs because these children's daddy ain't worth a damn, so any man stepping to me better have bank and be ready to raise some kids the right way or hit the highway,"** you might want to say something like, "Being a good mom is really important to me, and a part of being a good mom is making sure that my kids have a good father. I'm independent, but I realize how much better it would be for me and my family if a good man was in the picture.

Translation: You will have made clear that while you're quite capable of taking care of your own children, you recognize the importance of having a good man in the mix—something that will make a man who's willing to put in the work understand that he will be appreciated for being a good husband and father. And that's really all a man wants—a little appreciation every now and again.

Get the picture? Now, you've given us what we think is valuable information about the woman we're interested in. But more important, you've told us what your standards are, though you've done so by disguising them in a whole lot of pretty talk. It's like grape-flavored cough syrup; it's still medicine, but it's just going to taste better going down.

Now, I should add that while men appreciate it when women let them know up front what they require in a relationship, I firmly believe women need to step back every once in a while and let the man show you what he's made of—you know, prove that he's worthy of your time. I really do believe one of the biggest mistakes women make early on in the relationship is laying out in full detail all the things you love a man to do for you, without giving him a chance to show you what he's *willing* to do for you. I mean, it's nice and all that you like long walks by the beach, and chocolate on Valentine's Day, and you favor lilies in the summertime. But how, exactly, do you find out how creative, exciting, or giving a man is if you give him the blueprint for how to coax a smile on to your face, without requiring him to figure some of this out on his own? Be sure of this: if you tell a man you like red roses at work, dinner at that special restaurant across town, and Chanel bags for your birthday, that is exactly what he will give you—nothing less, but certainly nothing more. And you'll be happy about it—at first. But then give it about forty-five days or so, and he's going to stop doing what you told him you like because he'll have figured he did what he needed to do to get what he wanted. And you will think that because he stopped, he changed. And you'll go tell your girlfriends, "I don't know what happened—he used to do everything I like."

He did everything you like because you told him what you like.

My philosophy? Instead of telling him what you like, tell him what you *don't* like, and then see how he responds; let him research and dig and figure out how to get to your sweet spot. Just go right ahead and put it out there: "I'm not a fan of just sitting around in the house on the weekends," or "I don't like it when a man doesn't treat me like a lady," or "I don't like going to the same restaurants over and over again." Then, as your relationship progresses, watch his actions. For sure, you'll get his blueprint for how he conducts himself—you'll see what he's willing to give freely of his own accord. You don't like going to the same restaurants? He'll know to find new, interesting places to take you. You don't like sitting in the house on Saturdays? He'll be sure to take you out to a concert or a new museum exhibit, or he'll at least look through the newspaper and see what's going on around town so he has some suggestions for what you all can do together. He knows you don't like people who aren't family oriented? He's going to bring treats for the kids when he meets them, or even offer to take you and them to the park for a quick game of catch or a push on the swings, and no matter how uncomfortable he may think he might feel, he's going to go to the barbecue at your mom's house because he knows you require a man who likes and gets along with family. Sit back and watch him: see if he opens the car door for you, or pulls out your chair when you sit at the table, or turns off his phone when he's with you, so that he can dedicate all of his attention to your time together. And then if he doesn't step up to the plate—if he doesn't show you that he's willing to figure out how to put a smile on your face—then *you'll* be in the position to decide if he's capable of giving you what you need and at least some of what you want.

Of course, to lay out your requirements for a man, and convey the importance of following those requirements, you must first figure out what, exactly, your requirements are. I've listed questions here that you should consider as you formulate your top ten requirements, and I've left space for you to document your list:

1. What specific kind of man are you looking for?
   (For example, funny? Hardworking? Generous?)

   _____

   _____

   _____

2. How do you expect to be pursued? (Do you want
   regular phone calls? Text messages? Dates at least
   three times a week? Do you want him to always pick
   up the tab?)

   _____

   _____

   _____

3. What level of commitment do you expect? (Do you want an open relationship? Or to date exclusively? Should it be up for discussion?)

_____

_____

_____

4. What kind of financial security do you expect this man to have? (Do you want him to be rich? Do you want him to make more money than you? Are you okay with a blue-collar worker?)

_____

_____

_____

5. Do you want a man who wants kids and is family oriented?

_____

_____

_____

6. Does he have to be religious/spiritual?

_____

_____

_____

7. Do you mind if he's a divorcé or has kids?

_____

_____

_____

8. Can you help a man build his dream? Can you adapt
   to his plan?

   _____

   _____

   _____

9. What do you expect of his family? (Should you get
   along with his mother? Do you care if he doesn't get
   along with her? Or if his father was never around?)

   _____

   _____

   _____

10. What should he be willing to do to woo you? (Should
    he pursue you? Give you expensive gifts?)

    _____

    _____

    _____

10

THE FIVE QUESTIONS EVERY WOMAN SHOULD ASK BEFORE SHE GETS IN TOO DEEP

I had just gotten to Hollywood and I was seeing a lot of things my then thirty-eight-year-old eyes had never seen before. One of those that stood out most was the lifestyle of a famous and well-regarded celebrity, whose name I'm just going to go ahead and keep to myself. But this much I will tell you: this man had it all—money, fame, and a bevy of super-beauties so bad he could have easily made Hugh Hefner scratch his head and wonder how he could get in on *that* action. I mean this man was surrounded by gorgeous women. A lot. All. The. Time. And I was amazed at this because I couldn't understand how one person could get all of these fine women like this. I mean, he wasn't the best-looking dude in the business—there were others with more money, more prestige, and certainly better looks than him. Still, he was a master at keeping a stack of solid tens at all times, with commitments to none of them. I'd heard about these superplayers with supermodels on their arms and everything, but when I saw it up close, I was amazed at how the actual connections could happen, and especially why these women stayed with this guy, knowing that they were one of many hanging on his arm.

And I needed to know how this was done (um, not necessarily so that I, too, could have supermodels hanging on my every word, but because I was genuinely blown away by the phenomenon). So I sat down and talked to this guy and a bunch of other men who were in similar "relationships" and asked them point-blank: How do you keep these women coming back for more? And each one, including the most notorious of the bunch, laughed, shook his head, and said pretty much the same thing: those women want the money, the fame, and the lifestyle, and they're willing to put up with a lot of things—not many of them good—to get it. "But do they realize," I asked in all earnestness, "that this is going nowhere?" The one guy shook his head some more and said, simply, "They don't know where it's going because they never ask." He added: "What am I supposed to do—tell them I'm just using them for sex and arm candy? It just is what it is."

Blew me away.

And the more I asked the same questions of guys in similar situations, I heard the same answer, again and again. And each time I asked them what could have made it different for the women they were with, almost down to the letter, each one of those men said the same thing: if a woman came to me and quizzed me up front about my intentions, they would have known from the beginning that I'm not looking for anything serious. They don't ask, each one said, because they think they're going to run me off, so I get to just string them along. And the one celebrity who seemed to be the master of all of this said, quite simply, "I have enough of them so that when I get the questions, I don't have to answer because for every one woman who asks, I have two more who won't."

Call this what you want: foul; wrong; inexcusable—whatever. But that's how it is. And this kind of thinking from guys isn't just happening in celebrity circles, trust me. It happens with everyday guys—doctors and lawyers, truckers and deliverymen, too. Some of them have as many women as some of my celebrity friends, and the women they run game on are just as fine as some of the supermodels clinging to the arms of stars. But if you're a woman on a string of three or thirty-three, you're still on a string. And both you and I know that's not a good place to be.

Your objective is to avoid being on the string.

The first step, I think, is to get over the fear of losing a man by confronting him. Just stop being afraid, already. The most successful people in this world recognize that taking chances to get what they want is much more productive than sitting around being too scared to take a shot. The same philosophy can easily be applied to dating: if putting your requirements on the table means you risk him walking away, it's a risk you have to take. Because that fear can trip you up every time; all too many of you let the guy get away with disrespecting you, putting in minimal effort and holding out on the commitment to you because you're afraid he's going to walk away and you'll be alone again. And we men? We recognize this and play on it, big time. Know this: the game is old, and it's not ever going to change. My sons will do it the same way because they can and there will be women who allow it to happen. But you can certainly know the rules up front, and change up your strategy, so *you* don't get played.

How do you do this? Start by making the man be really clear *up front* about what he wants out of his life and his relationship with you. You do this by asking him these key five questions—questions that will help you determine right away what values this guy has and how you fit into his plans. I devised these questions after years of watching men play women, and women falling for it, and constantly asking myself and even some of my friends who are masters at the game, "If I were a woman, how could I avoid all of this?" They're great questions, too—the answers will tell you everything you need to know about this guy in your life or the guy you hope to have in your life. Asking these questions will help you determine whether you should stick around to see where your relationship goes, or if you should run really fast in the opposite direction. Note: There's no need to delay asking these questions—ask them right away, as soon as you think you might be remotely attracted to a man you've met. If he's turned off by the questions, so what: you have the right to the information. And if he isn't willing to answer them, well you know from the gate he's not the one for you.

So let's just get started with the questions. Remember: No. Fear.

QUESTION NO. 1:
WHAT ARE YOUR SHORT-TERM GOALS?

If you're going to get into a relationship with a man, you should know what his plans are and how they fit into the key elements that make a man—who he is, what he does, and how much he makes. These three things, as I've already told you, are extremely important to any mature, grown man, and you have every right to know what he's doing right now, and what he's planning over the next three to five years, to be the real, grown man he wants to be. His answer also will help you determine whether you want to be a part of that plan or not. You'll know to throw up your much-needed red flag if he doesn't have a plan at all.

If he's got a plan, well great. Act like you're superinter-ested and ask follow-up questions—be the inquisitive, en-thusiastic detective that you are. Men love to talk about themselves. We do this because we know that in order to catch you, we have to impress you. So allow us to impress. The more inquisitive and interested you are, the more infor-mation he'll give you. Say things like, "Wow, how did you get into that field?" or "How interesting—what does it take to make that successful?" And listen carefully. The whole time he's talking, you should be evaluating whether he's ac-tually working hard to meet his goals or if he's a lazy dreamer just talking a whole lot of nonsense. You should also be fig-uring out if you see yourself in that short-term plan; if you know what his plan is, you can immediately assess if you want to be part of it and what role you can play in it, or if you need to remove yourself from that equation. For in-stance, if he says, "I'm a technician for the cable company, but I'm going to college at night to earn my B.A. in engi-neering so that I can move up the ranks at my job," then you know this guy has a plan and he's executing it. Maybe you can even see yourself helping him study or being there for him at graduation and giving him suggestions for how to transform himself from the blue-collar worker who installs the cable to the engineer who helps build the technology for the cable company. The point is, he has a plan and he's work-ing toward it, which means that he's trying to be the man he wants to be—the kind that just might fit in line with what you're looking for in a good, solid mate.

But if you ask him what his short-term goals are, and he tells you something crazy, like "I'm in street pharmaceuticals, and right now I have one block but my goal in the next few years is to have ten blocks on the west side from Henry Street to Brown Street," well, then you know right then and there that you can go on ahead and keep it moving. The same applies to the man who states his short-term goals, but clearly has no plan to implement them. For instance, if he says his dream is to be a producer, but he's not doing anything in the field to actually become one—he's not interning or working for a film company, he's not writing or reading any scripts, he's not making any connections in the industry that might open some doors for him, he hasn't worked for four months and has no prospects of a job in the field he says he's interested in—then you know this man doesn't have a plan. And if he doesn't have a plan, he's not going to achieve his short-term goal—or it's really not a goal, he's just talking out of his behind. Either way, you may not want to sign up for his plan. Just stick to your own. Sure, there's a chance that he might get it together and make it in the industry, but why do you have to sign up for that? If he's got this whole pie-in-the-sky dream, figure out if he's lying there looking at the stars, or if he's got a jet pack strapped to his back and he's about to take off to go grab that dream.

QUESTION NO. 2:
WHAT ARE YOUR LONG-TERM GOALS?

Trust me on this: a man who really has a vision for where he wants to see himself in ten years has looked into his future and seriously considered what it'll take for him to get there. It means he has foresight, and he's plotting out the steps to his future. If he says something silly like "I'm just trying to make it day by day," run. If his long-term plan is the same as his short-term plan, get out. Immediately. Because his answer tells you that he hasn't thought his life through, or he doesn't see you in it and so he has no reason to divulge the details to you. All he's got for you is game. If he doesn't have a plan, why do you want him to stick around, anyway?

The man you should consider spending a little time on is the one who has a plan—a well-thought-out plan that you can see yourself in. Because please believe me when I tell you—and like I told you in an earlier chapter—a man always has a plan. I know I did when I first started working as a comedian. I knew before I even told my first joke in front of an audience that within the next five years, my goal was to become a headliner and make at least $2,500 a week. With my eye on that prize, I was soon making $2,500 a week, and happy about it, too. Still, I wanted to become a headliner, and I upped the ante: now I wanted to make $5,000 to $7,500 per week. It took me about eight years, but I managed to meet my financial goal—and I was happy about that, too.

And then I met Sinbad.

Now at the time, Sinbad was working at a comedy club in Birmingham, where he'd become so large, he was making $50,000 to $70,000 a week at this one particular club. Every. Seven. Days. And I knew I wanted a piece of that action. His success made me realize that there was something to this comedy thing—that I needed to set in place a long-term plan that would afford me the kind of life I could see was possible for a comedian. I wanted to get on *television* to provide a life-style for my family that would make them proud. I envisioned my life this way, and then created a plan for how I was going to get it. Now, I knew it wasn't going to be easy—that it would take time, because there were very few comedy clubs where you could make that kind of money, and you had to have the right connections and a great team to help get you there. But the point is, I had a long-term plan, with steps on how I was going to get there. Eventually, I reached those goals and then some.

Once you hear your potential mate's answer to questions number one and number two, you'll have a firm understanding of the kind of man you're dealing with. Do not tie your life together with a human being who does not have a plan, because you'll find out that if he's not going anywhere, sooner or later, you'll be stuck, too.

QUESTION NO. 3:
WHAT ARE YOUR VIEWS ON RELATIONSHIPS?

Now this one is a multiple-part question that sizes up how a man feels about a gamut of relationships—from how he feels about his parents and kids to his connection with God. Each answer will reveal a lot more about him—whether he's serious about commitment, the kind of household in which he was raised, what kind of father and husband he might be, whether he knows the Lord, all of that. And the only way you'll find out the answers to these questions is to ask. Do it before you kiss this man, maybe even before you agree to go on a date with him—this is a great phone conversation, for sure. And don't be shy or nervous about asking these questions, either, because what are you supposed to be doing with this man if not talking to him? If he has a problem talking about this right here, then something's wrong. Run.

First, find out how he feels about family. What are his views on it? Does he want a family? How does he feel about children? If you have a child, tell your man about him or her—it's his business to know, but more important, it's your business to find out if he sees himself being a father. If he doesn't want kids and you do, then you can stop all of this right now. (Please know that if a man says he doesn't want kids, he's probably not going to change his mind, regardless of the intensity of his feelings for you.) Moreover, if he doesn't like kids and you already have them, where, exactly, is this relationship going?

Next, ask him about his relationship with his mother. It's the first relationship a man has with a woman, and if he has a good track record with her, then chances are he knows how to treat a woman with respect and has some kind of idea of how to profess, provide, and protect not only a woman but a potential family, too. I don't know a boy living whose mother isn't beloved. We learn to protect her and provide for her; we learn about the basic core of love for a woman from her. Indeed, if a man is at odds with his mother, it's a safe bet that he's going to be at odds with you. If you hear any part of "Man, me and my mother? We just don't get along . . ." in his answer, erase his number and texts from your phone and keep it moving.

After you find out how he feels about his mother, ask him about his father. If he had a great relationship with his dad, then he was probably raised with a core set of values that he'll bring to your potential home together. Now, I understand that a whole host of men grew up without fathers in their households, but chances are that the man you're interested in had a male role model in his life who showed him the ropes of manhood, or perhaps the absence of his own father taught him a few things about what he doesn't want to do when he becomes a father. At any rate, ask questions about his relationship with his father, and his answers are bound to reveal the kind of father he just might turn out to be.

You're also going to have to ask him about his relationship with God. Let me be direct: if you meet a man who doesn't have a relationship with God, he doesn't go to church and has no intention of ever going, and he has no belief system he can point to as a guiding force in his life, then it's a problem. After all, what moral barometer does he answer to if not to God? What's going to make him even consider being loyal to you? What's going to make him do right by you and the kids? What's going to make him feel whole? I'm not saying that you shouldn't date a man who doesn't go to church, or who has a different belief system than you. But if his core beliefs don't match up with yours, you're likely to have a problem.

These next two questions should be asked after you've been talking and dating for a while. Ideally, ask them before you have parted with the cookie (y'all know what I mean). If you have already had a sexual encounter with the man, you can ask these questions anyway. The answers may hurt a little bit more, but at least you'll know.

QUESTION NO. 4: WHAT DO YOU THINK ABOUT ME?

Now, this one you'll have to ask after a few dates, because he's going to need time to get to know you. But his answer will be critical because it will reveal to you what his plans for you are. If you've been out on a couple of dates and you've had lots of conversation, you know something about him, but what's more important, you want to know what he is thinking about you. You have a right to know. Oh, trust me, he thought *something* about you when he first walked up to you, and you need to know what it is. He was attracted to something—he liked your hair, your eyes, your legs, your outfit. He didn't walk over there just to be walking. Beyond the initial attraction, however, men pretty much know if you're the kind of woman they're going to sleep with and keep it moving, or if they're going to stick around and see if they want more. This, you will be able to tell by his answers.

Listen to his answer closely. I assure you this is how it will go, because every man will answer this question the same exact way: "I think you're great, I think you'd make a great mom, you're fun, kind, you're really beautiful, you turn me on, you're energetic, outgoing, a hard worker, very smart. I think you're the kind of woman I could see myself with," all of that generic stuff we know you want to hear. Still, this isn't the answer you should be looking for. You want specifics. You want to know that he's really thought about you beyond the surface. So do the follow-ups. "Oh, you think I'm kind? What about me makes you think I'm kind?" Then sit back and listen. If he can't give you a concrete example of how you've shown your kindness, he's not really thinking about you beyond the surface. But if he says, "You remember that time when it was my mom's birthday and you called me and reminded me to pick up a card for her? That was really nice." If he tells you he thinks you're a great mom, make him tell you what it is about you

that makes you a great mom. And so forth with whatever char-
acteristic he attributes to you. The level of his specifics will
give you yet another clue into this man's intentions for your
relationship. If he can give you specifics, it means he's been
listening and adding it up—he's determining if he's going to
keep you, if he can see himself in a committed relationship
with you. And that could mean that you're at least on the same
relationship page.

QUESTION NO. 5:
HOW DO YOU *FEEL* ABOUT ME?

Now this is not to be confused with what do you "think"
about me—"think" and "feel" are two wholly different things.
And if a man cannot tell you how he feels about you after a
month of dating, it's because he doesn't feel anything for
you—he just wants something. Ask a man how he feels about
you, and he's going to get confused and nervous: "I told you
before—I think you're . . ." he begins. You cut him right off
and say, "No, no, I want to know how you *feel* about me." He
might shift in his chair, scratch his head, light a cigar—anything to get out of giving you an answer or thinking of what he
thinks you want him to say. But you'll have to get him to
answer it.

Don't get upset if he doesn't answer right away: he's got to go into that part of himself that he doesn't like to go to, and that's the emotional part. Men do not do emotion well, at all, and expressing it doesn't come easy. He can answer questions about God and the kids and his mother, but with this question, you're asking him to look into his soul, and our DNA isn't made up for the heartfelt outpouring to just anybody. But this doesn't mean you should let up. What you're looking for in his answer is something like this: "When I don't see you, I miss talking to you, I always wonder what you're doing and whenever you come around, I just feel better—you're the type of woman I've been trying to find." In other words, his answer has to make you feel wonderful. He may not be in love with you just yet, but he's crazy about you and he's probably thinking he wants to explore a long-term commitment with you, because when he starts to profess and put you in a position where he can provide for and protect you, he's seeing a future with you in it. And this is exactly where you want to be with this guy.

The "I think you're cool" answer isn't going to cut it here, ladies. And if, after you've asked the question and probed deeper, you realize his feelings for you don't run very deep—that he's just not there—then you need to not be there, too. Pump the brakes until you start hearing and feeling from him the things that you think are important to hear and feel from a man with whom you're willing to forge a relationship.

*W*e men are fully aware that we have to answer these questions, and any real man is going to answer them. You may not necessarily like the answers, but he's going to answer them. If he refuses, then don't bother with him. Don't think that you're going to work it out later—that you'll wait him out until he gets more comfortable with you—because that would be nothing more than blind hope. Before you know it, you'll be finding out the hard way that this isn't the guy for you, and you'll be starting all the conversations with your girlfriends like this: "You know, I slept with him and he's not about anything, I don't even know if he likes kids. . . ." Don't let this happen. Empower yourself—it's your right to know all of these answers up front; per my ninety-day rule, which you'll discover in the next chapter, you need to ask these questions within the first few months of a courtship.

If you're already in a relationship with someone, these questions are still valid if you don't know the answers. You can ask them for clarification. Or you may need to ask them with the hope that they'll solidify what you may already know—either that you need to get out of your relationship or that you are headed in the right direction. His answers may help you cut your losses, before you invest too many more years in a relationship that isn't going the way you want it to go. Or they may make you say, "Wow, I'm glad I'm with this man."

Know, too, that though we'll answer the questions because

we like talking about ourselves, our answers just may make us consider the woman who's asking the questions in a different light. We definitely want to know where our women stand on these issues, too, but we're not going to bring it up—especially if our intentions for you aren't pure. But in your conversations around these issues, your man just might learn something about you, too, something that makes him know he's got a pretty solid woman on his side. Say, for instance, he tells you that he wants to be an engineer and he's going to night school to get his degree, and you tell him that you have a few friends who are engineers and you can offer to introduce him to them so that they can give some helpful advice as he works toward his new career. When you offer that helping hand, he starts to think, "Wow, this woman is interested in my goals and ambitions. She's offering to help me out. Maybe she might be the one to get me to the next level." And he might just envision including you in those "next level" plans.

See, you're getting information from him and plugging yourself into all these slots—do I see myself in his short-term plans, his long-term plans, as a part of his family, having babies with him, helping him continue a solid relationship with his mom, being a role-model dad for our kids, the whole picture? But it's a two-way street: know that this guy you're quizzing is listening to these intelligent, inquisitive questions, and calculating whether you're a woman who is his keeper or just a sports fish.

11

THE NINETY-DAY RULE

Getting the Respect You Deserve

Nineteen seventy-seven—it was a good year. I was living in Cleveland, I had a two-bedroom apartment, brand spanking new. I hadn't quite gotten the car I wanted, but I was working on it. And I had a job at the Ford motor plant. They had a high hourly wage there, and overtime—more money than a man of my stature could dream of making. But more important, Ford had benefits. Thing is, you had to be on the job for a while to get them. Oh, you could get a paycheck, but you could not get the benefits; and as far as any of the full-time regulars on the line were concerned, you were not *in* until you had the benefits. Ford's policy was that you had to work at least ninety days before they'd cover your health insurance; this was the plant management saying to me, we will provide you benefits after you have proven to me you are worthy—work hard, show up on time, follow your supervisor's orders, and get along with your co-workers for ninety days, and then you can get dental and medical coverage. You can get your eyes checked, no problem. Your hernia could bust and we will take care of you. We will take care of your kids' teeth and eyes, and if you've got a woman, she can get glasses and crowns on her teeth if she needs them, and any more babies you have with your lady after this, we're going to take care of them, too. Your whole family will be covered. We are going to provide you with a benefit package.

And you know something? All of this made perfect sense to me. I was being challenged to show everybody at the plant that I was serious, and ready and able to work hard for both the salary and the right to have them pay my medical and dental expenses—and as a man, I needed and wanted to prove that I was up for the challenge and worthy of the reward. I agreed 100 percent with what the Ford Motor Company was saying to me, and so I signed on the dotted line. I wanted to be a part of the Ford family.

The first day I got paid, the supervisor came through and said, "Here's your check, appreciate you coming." The check was cool, but I wasn't making an appointment at the doctor's office anytime soon. If I got a toothache—hell, if both of my front teeth were loose and about to fall clean out of my mouth—there wouldn't be any dentist appointments for ninety days, because Ford had already said I had to prove myself to the people who signed the checks in order to get the extras—the perks.

It was a really simple equation: work hard, prove yourself, get the benefits.

And guess what? It's the same way with jobs in the government, places like the post office, the DMV—and even in some corporations. You have got to prove yourself to get the good stuff, the extras, the benefits.

So if Ford and the government won't give a man benefits until he's been on the job and proven himself, why, ladies, are you passing out benefits to men before they've proven themselves worthy? Come on now, you know what the *benefits* are. I'm not talking about being nice to him, or cooking for him, or going out to dinner with him, or helping him pick out an outfit, or bringing him around your mother. Those are things that happen during the course of a budding relationship—you do special things for each other because you care. By benefits, in case you haven't figured it out, I'm talking about sex. And if you're giving your benefits to a guy who's only been on the job for a week or two, you're making a grave mistake.

You don't know this man—not much about him, anyway.

He doesn't know you.

He hasn't proven himself.

And he could walk off the job at any time.

And you'll have no one but yourself to blame.

Think about it: the first guy you slept with quicker than ninety days—where is he? I'm willing to bet that you're probably not with him. True, there are some people out there somewhere who had sex early in the relationship and are still together to this very day, but that's rare. More likely than not, a guy who gets benefits early in a relationship, without having to put in work or prove himself, leaves and moves on to a committed relationship with a woman who puts him through some type of probationary period to find out more about him. I'm sure that woman laid out the rules—the requirements—early on, and let her intended know that he could either rise up to those requirements, or just move on.

A directive like that signals to a man that you are not a plaything—someone to be used and discarded. It tells him that what you have—your benefits—are special, and that you need time to get to know him and his ways to decide if he *deserves* them. The man who is willing to put in the time and meet the requirements is the one you want to stick around, because that guy is making a conscious decision that he, too, has no interest in playing games and will do what it takes to not only stay on the job, but also get promoted and be the proud beneficiary of your benefits. And you, in the meantime, win the ultimate prize of maintaining your dignity and self-esteem, and earning the respect of the man who recognized that you were worth the wait.

Of course, you've got to use your ninety days wisely; a probationary period means nothing if you're not putting this guy through the paces. During that ninety-day period, you should be checking him out—does he come when he says he's going to come; does he call when he's going to be late; does he like and care about your friends and, if you have them, your children; does he express his joy at being in your presence? Most important, is this really a man with whom you can see yourself in a committed relationship? Or do you see signs that make your God-given intuition kick in? You know how it goes: you haven't been invited over to his house, you only have the cell phone number, he won't answer his phone when you're in the room or he takes hushed calls in the corner where you can't hear what's being said—he tells you he's dating other women, or, somehow, you just know he is. These are tendencies you can't possibly see in a man you've dated for less than ninety days because guess what? The guy who is dating you just to get the benefits up front is going to be on his best behavior in the beginning, specifically so he can make you think he's worthy. But just as sure as time is going to come and go, he'll eventually show his true nature.

Give it at least ninety days, and you can smoke all of that out of him, so that you can be sure that this guy is the right man for you. After all, it's your right to want what you want—and to actually get it. Put yourself first: ask the five questions (as mentioned in the previous chapter), withhold the benefits, and demand the respect. If you have a high level of respect for yourself, you're automatically going to command that respect from a man. Make him qualify for the benefits, and I guarantee you'll have a better man on your hands—and in your bed. And once you're satisfied he's worthy of the benefits, you can pass it out like sandwiches at a picnic.

Hold on, I know what you're thinking: you're thinking that if he doesn't get sex from you, he'll go and get it somewhere else, and you will have lost out on that one chance to get him to be your man—or he'll think you're playing games if you make him wait, and he'll move on to the next woman who's willing to take him into her bed.

Wrong.

In fact, one of those mind tricks we've been playing on women since the beginning of time is to convince you all that waiting doesn't matter, that giving it up early and quick is the way to go. Listen to me: if we could convince you that you should strip naked and get to it within the first five minutes of our first meeting, we would. This is not a secret: men love and want sex, and will try (within reason) to get it by any means necessary.

But guess what? He. Can. Wait. Yes, of course you run the risk of scaring him off, but isn't the guy who sleeps with you without any obligation to you, or consideration of your wants, needs, and emotional well-being, the one you *want* to go away? Isn't reserving something that special for a man who earns it more of a benefit *to you*? You have the power to *make him wait*—

to prove to you that he deserves your love and affection. The Power. Just think of it this way: when it comes to having sex with a woman, we men don't decide a thing. We don't determine when we're going to sleep with you—that decision is yours. The decision of when we get to kiss you is yours. When we let go of each other's hug and embrace? That decision is yours. We put our hands somewhere on your body other than your shoulder and *you* decide if we can keep touching that place or if we gotta let it go. Our job is to convince you to give it to us—to allow us to touch it, let us have it. But the decision on whether we actually get to have it is Y.O.U.R.S.

Don't give up that power. Keep it. You only give up that power when the man has earned it, and he is going to respect it and do something with it.

That's the truth.

Women have crumbled empires with that power. Cleopatra helped destroy Rome. Read your Bible: we're still in a jam right now because of Eve. Women have always had that kind of power, and you do, too—including making the man you're dating wait for the benefits. Oh, I'm not saying you can't pay the man; payment comes along the way during that ninety-day probationary period. You can hug, kiss, talk on the phone, go for a walk in the park, have an ice cream cone together, go out for dinner. Your time is a form of payment. When we're out to dinner with you, you can't imagine how we feel when we're looking forward to meeting you and you show up with your lip gloss shining, your eyes seductively made up, and your hair—whether it's blown out, in a weave, or natural—is lovely, and your body gleaming. I cannot tell you the fulfillment we have in knowing that we've secured your time. And to be seen in public with you is a bonus; it's all the affirmation we need. The payment is incredible.

Hugging? Payment.

Kissing? Payment.

You getting dressed up? Payment.

Going out with us? Payment.

Exchanging explicit e-mails? Payment.

But if he wants to sleep with you—make babies and have a family? Those are benefits.

So he's got ninety days on the job to prove himself worthy—ninety days in which you can figure this man out. You're an investigator—can't nobody find stuff out like a woman. Y'all put the police to shame, make the little investigative tricks they show on *CSI* and *Law & Order: SVU* look like counting lessons on *Sesame Street*. You know how to find stuff out about a man he may not have even known about himself. So get to it. Create some scenarios so you can figure out just who this guy is, and whether he's good enough for your benefits. Here are a few things you might want to find out.

How does he react when you tell him you've got some problems?

Maybe your car broke down, or the water heater is about to give its last breath, or your kids are acting up and you can't get a handle on them. You're exhausted and the stress is showing on your face—he can hear it in your voice. If he asks you, "What's the matter?" that's a good start. He's been around you long enough to know when you're not your normal self. That's progress. But now, if you answer him with, "My car broke down and I don't have the money to fix it right now so I'm just a little worried about how I'm going to get to work tomorrow," and he says, "Okay, well, call me when you figure it out," you can scratch him off the benefits list. Be clear: you're not asking him for money to get the car fixed. You're just trying to see if he's going to probe deeper, and find out if there's anything he can do to help, whether it's to give you some advice on how to fix the problem, or step in to help you fix it. Did he offer to get up an hour earlier so he could drive you to work while your car is in the shop? Or give you the number to a guy who can fix your car for a deep discount? Did he offer to get up under the hood and take a look himself? Or tell you about his friend who owns a car shop and might be willing to do a favor for him—and you?

Real men extend themselves to women they care about. If you have a problem and your man does not extend himself—he doesn't try to make it better—this is not a good candidate for benefits.

Now that other man, the one who'll scoot on the ground on his back with the toolbox, and come back out hours later with car grease all over his shirt and hands and face from trying to fix your raggedy car? That's the one who might deserve a cold beer and later on, some benefits.

How does your man react under pressure?

Let's say an ex of yours is starting to call again, and it's making you uncomfortable because the breakup was particularly nasty and you just don't want to go down that road with him again. You tell the new guy you're bothered by this and are not sure how to make the ex just go away. A benefits-worthy man will immediately launch into "fix-it" mode—he will see what he can do to (a) stop the guy from calling, and (b) get you to feel safe again. He might tell you something like, "Next time he calls, let me talk to him." That's a little extreme, but there are some men who will get on the line and let the last ex know to mind his place. Or your new man may give you suggestions for how to deal with the unwanted phone calls; he might tell you to block his number or put a special ring on the phone so you know who it is when the phone rings, maybe even give you a few words to say to this guy to make him stop calling. This is a pressure situation; it doesn't require an action, but a reaction. If the new guy says something like, "I just can't get into all of this," then he's not a good candidate for benefits. You're going to be in pressure situations in your relationship time and time again, and you should know up front, right now, if this guy is ready to handle it. If he goes into protect or fix-it mode, then he envisions you as his woman. And he just might be worth the benefits.

How does he react to bad news?

Say you lose a loved one—someone really close to you. A man who has plans for you will immediately offer some form of comfort and help so that you can take the time to grieve. He might ask you if he can take your kids out for a couple of hours so you can have some time to yourself, or he might ask you if he can go with you to the funeral home to be with you while you see about the funeral arrangements, and so that he can express his condolences to your family. Note, ladies, he's probably not going to want to sit there and let you retrace your childhood and reminisce about the first time your deceased loved one pushed you on the swing; that's not about to happen—it's not what men do. But a real man will respond with some kind of solution—he will do what he can to help you stop crying, because no man wants to see his woman crying. If this man is not comforting—if he's not coming up with some solutions to help you feel better, then he needs to be fired. He has no rights to the benefits.

A man who is worthy of the benefits will be there for you no matter what bad circumstance comes along. If you lose your job or fall behind on some payments because you had a huge and unexpected financial situation to deal with, he'll recognize your need for help and rise to the occasion, whether it's giving you a little extra cash to make the minimum payment on your bills, stopping by with a few bags of groceries, or filling your gas tank.

How does he react when he's told "no"?

Let's just get right to the crux of this whole chapter: when a man asks for sex, and he is told no, his reaction to that no will tell you everything you need to know about him. If the phone calls cease or become infrequent, the flowers stop coming, the dating slows down, please understand that this man was just in it for the sex. If he says something stupid, such as, "I don't need to wait for sex—I can get it from anybody," you tell him right back, "Please do." This cuts the riffraff away right away. But if your saying no doesn't deter him, and he continues to try to get to know you better and prove to you that he's worthy of your benefits, then he's really, truly interested in you. Don't get me wrong: he's still interested in the sex. But he's also interested in knowing how you feel and what time frame you're working on. Then the relationship becomes about what you want—what your needs are. And that's what you're after, right?

It's that simple.

Now, I realize that ninety days sounds like a lot of time and you kinda need to be real creative to keep his attention on you and your new relationship. So I came up with a list of things you can do with your man to help you—and him—stay focused on the relationship.

1. Go on dates that help you find out each other's interests: if he's into photography, hit up a photography exhibit at the local museum; if you're into cooking, take a cooking class together.

2. Host a barbecue at your house and invite him to meet your friends and family; a good guy should be comfortable meeting the people you love.

3. Go to church together; know that he's interested.

4. Sign up for a sexy Latin dance class so you can learn some new moves—it'll show you if he's into trying new things, and you can tell if the man has, um, rhythm.

5. Go out for a picnic in the park with the kids; see if he's comfortable with them.

6. Find out each other's favorite artists and attend a concert together.

7. Release your inner kid and spend an evening playing games at an arcade.

8. Have a few "firsts" together—go horseback riding together, or hit up a batting cage, or fall all over each other at the ice skating rink.

9. Volunteer together—help out at a local soup kitchen or read books to kids at a local foster home; you can tell a lot about a man who's willing to help others.

10. Rent a convertible and get lost cruising in your city; you'll have plenty of time to talk on a long drive.

11. Find a quiet place where you can watch the sunset together.

12. Play a board game.

13. Go for a long walk under a starlit sky.

14. Send each other naughty e-mails, so he can be sure that when he does get it, it's going to be good. (And you can make sure he's literate while you're at it.)

15. Read a passage out of each other's favorite books.

16. Have a movie night in which you both bring your favorite DVDs.

17. Go to a record store and listen to each other's favorite artists.

18. Challenge each other to do something silly, like build a sandcastle at the beach or a game of jacks or marbles.

19. Hit up a comedy show; you can learn a lot about a person by what they find funny and what they think is offensive.

12

IF HE'S MEETING THE KIDS
AFTER YOU DECIDE HE'S "THE ONE,"
IT'S TOO LATE

L et's get one thing straight. When a man approaches you, he doesn't see anything except what's in front of him—how you're fitting into your jeans, what the shape of your leg looks like in those heels, how your lips look with that lip gloss shining, how beautiful your eyes are with all those colors around them. We don't care if you use M.A.C or Bobbi Brown, Maybelline or L'Oréal. We don't care anything about where you live, who you used to be with, what kind of car you're driving, how much money you're making and spending, or even who you're spending it on. And we especially don't consider whether you have kids and what that would mean if we were in a relationship with you. In fact, if we're about game and our game goes right, we never make it to the kids; we figure we're going to have dinner a couple of times, maybe catch a movie or go bowling, and be in a room with a bed frame and a mattress in it in a matter of days if our game is proper, or a few weeks if you're playing hard to get. Kids? Please. Some men don't care any which way about your kids. The guy you're trying to hook up with won't be any more interested in your life as a mother than what color toenail polish you'll ask for at your next pedicure appointment. In fact, if a guy is in it for one thing—if he's a game runner looking for nothing more than your cookie—then the plan is to *never meet the kids*. And once he gets what he was looking for, oh, you can believe he'll be plotting how to move on.

What's most likely to happen is you'll follow the time-honored single mom tradition of dating a guy, all the while keeping him as far away from your home life as possible—partly because you want to get clarity on the relationship and the direction in which it's moving, partly because you don't want to introduce your kids to any man unless you're absolutely, 100 percent sure that he's in it for the long haul. Once you've convinced yourself there's long-term potential with the guy in question, *then* you invite him home to meet the kids.

Stop right there.

I'm here to tell you that you're going about this all the way wrong. You can't become emotionally attached to this man and make some kind of verbal or, especially, physical commitment to him, and then finally drag him to the house only to find out he doesn't like your kids, and your kids don't like him. You've gone and got this guy all hot and bothered thinking you're some sexy vixen who's fun and interesting and wild and willing and able to swing from chandeliers, and once you walk into your living room, he's tripping over Tonka trucks and mashing crayons into the carpet while your kids are begging for potato chips, crying loudly, and telling you the baby's diaper needs changing? This is not a good situation, ladies. Not a good situation at all. In fact, the introduction is late—much too late.

See, a man needs to be able to see what all he's going to be responsible for up front; if he sees you in the role as a mother, he's going to immediately try to figure out if he sees himself in the role as a father. He's going to evaluate if he can afford those children, if he wants to be bothered with the drama that comes when a baby's daddy is likely lurking in the background, whether he can handle any animosity that might come his way when the kids get wind of him, and, finally, if he wants to play second fiddle to the children, whose needs you surely will meet many moons before his—all of these things and then some will be taken into account. And if you hold back key information he needs to assess his potential life together with you, and pop it on him when he's not expecting it, he's not going to receive the information well—plain and simple. In fact, he's likely to think he was duped—duped into thinking he had one woman, when clearly he's involved with someone who comes with a whole different set of obligations, responsibilities, and potential requirements. (Note: Telling him you have kids is *not* good enough.)

Besides that, the longer you hold off introducing him to the kids, the more he's going to think there's something wrong with them—that you're hiding the kids for a reason. And that will only make him more apprehensive about that initial meeting; in his mind, you will have elevated the get-together to the level of a G8 summit, giving the introduction way more power than it needs or deserves. He's meeting the kids, for goodness' sake—they're not sitting down to a state dinner at the White House.

So, to avoid all of this, you need to get the kids in the game early; a natural, casual introduction early in the relationship will set all of you up for a much healthier connection. He should be sitting across the room or at the park or at the ice cream parlor with those kids right around the time you start developing emotional feelings for this guy beyond "I'm attracted to him." If you're starting to wonder whether this guy is right for you, then you might as well see if he's right for the kids. Let him see you and them in your natural setting—in a mother-child capacity. He should see you feeding oatmeal and fruits to the toddler, and braiding the seven-year-old's hair, and folding the ten-year-old's laundry, and cheering the fifteen-year-old on during football practice. He'll be looking at all of these things to determine what kind of mother you are, and whether he'd like to have you be the mother of his children. This is hugely important, ladies, because we men recognize that some women aren't cut out to be mothers—that there's no automatic mothering gene that kicks in for women just because she has the equipment to carry and birth babies. Just as some women can't drive, just as some women can't do math, just as some women can't cook, some women aren't good at mothering. And a guy wants to see that the potential mother of his children is at least decent at it, that she can be kind, compassionate, creative, and stern. He wants to see that you can handle matters without unraveling—that the stress that comes with marriage and family is something you can handle with decent skill—because the one thing we men do know is that marriage and family equals stress. So we're looking—looking to see if you can handle having to make dinner for the kids, while helping one with the homework, tending to the other who's had the flu for a week, helping one get on the Internet, and kicking the other off the Internet's inappropriate sites, all at the same time, without strangling anybody.

More important, you should introduce the kids to the man you're dating so that you can see him in a fatherly capacity. Walk him into your house, introduce him to little Taylor and Brianna, and then sit back and observe; you will get the purest and truest reaction from him when you do this. If he actually knows something about kids and likes them, he'll be able to start and hold a conversation with a six-year-old; the biggest test of someone's children skills is whether they can talk to kids in a way that will keep them engaged and elicit a response. If he freezes up and acts like he's on the witness stand—he just can't think of anything to say or ask—then chances are his intense reaction is a sign he's just not all that good with children. Similarly, if he's completely defenseless against the powers of the wicked little kids who are liked by no one but their mother, then that's a potential problem, too. The guy who can't hold his own in those situations—who can't use humor or compassion or square his shoulders in a take-charge way to deflect any attempts by the kids to do damage or harm to him—may have some issues, too. After all, you want your potential man to be able to be, well, a man around your kids—someone who can take charge when the kids act like fools and they need a man to set them straight. Kids, after all, respect authority.

All of this, of course, will tell you a lot about this guy—about the kind of father he'd be. If he's comfortable with the kids, can entertain as well as give them advice, and give you solid advice on how to troubleshoot, too, then he's showing you the traits of a potentially good father figure for your child. Likewise, when he sees you with your children—nurturing them, feeding them, and keeping all of their needs satisfied, you're showing him not only that you're a good mother to your own children, but that you're potential mother material for any children he already has, and any babies you two might make together.

Sure, how your kids feel about this guy should count for something, too. Children have an uncanny ability to pick up on when human beings mean them well or harm; if they're younger, they have no ulterior motives about not liking someone, especially if you introduce him as "my friend Mr. So-and-So," just like you would any female friend of yours. But know, too, that if your child's father is in your kid's life, your child may not necessarily have the most warm and fuzzy feelings about the new guy—and that's natural. In these cases, your child isn't exactly going to make it easy for the new man to get close quickly. But this isn't necessarily going to scare a man off. (First off, how would a grown man look being scared off by a child? If he runs, let him.) Oh, the new guy might raise an eyebrow or two if he keeps running into problems with Little Chucky—if on the first date, Chucky forgoes a handshake for a swift kick to the shin, and on the second date, the little monster purposely rides his bicycle up the side of the new man's ride, and on the third date, he "accidentally" spills his fruit punch all over your man's nice white linen suit. But if you're worth it, he's going to stick it out and see if Chucky is truly insane, or if he simply keeps catching him on his bad days. He'll try harder to win Chucky over, and give the relationship more time to assess whether Chucky is bearable.

And teenagers? Oh, men don't even see them as a problem; no man walks into a situation thinking they're going to be best friends with the teenager in the house. Even their biological parents can't stand teenagers, and vice versa, sometimes, so the odds are low that the new man is going to have a kumbaya moment with a sulking, hulking, attitudinal older child. The beauty of teenagers, though, is that they tend to make themselves invisible. As a result, your new man might actually be able to focus on your relationship without the distraction of a misbehaving kid. But a man who genuinely wants to be in your life will try to be a part of your teenager's life—he won't be deterred. He's expecting that a teenager will be a jerk to him. What he'll try to determine is whether the jerkiness is an act to be mean, or if that's truly who this kid is.

Now, we all understand your need as a mother to protect the emotions of your children and your reluctance to let them get attached to someone you can't guarantee won't disappear and take your kids' hearts with him. Likewise, we understand how important it is for you to not look like you're fast and loose, running men all through the house like your living room is a bus stop. We also know this violates every single rule you've had hammered into your head about such introductions. But my goodness, I'm not talking about bringing everybody to the house. I'm talking about the guy that you think might be serious about you. And don't worry about whether he's going to think you're trying to trap him or you're just looking for some sucker to take up where your kids' daddy failed. Single moms all over the planet have convinced themselves, with their natural instincts as nurturers and protectors in full gear, that bringing men they've just met around the kids is unsafe. But, ladies, here's a secret: that's exactly what the players who wrote the rule book you've been following want you to believe. Women live under that fear because the men intent on playing the game tricked you into thinking this way; as long as you believe it, we get to keep the game alive until we get what we want, without any obligations.

If you really want a good man in your life, if you've asked God to give you a family, you've got to stop all this foolishness and introduce this man to your kids so you can figure him out. The sincere men among us know that women with kids are a package deal, and we'll understand that you are a mother with obligations to your kids first, especially if you lay that out up front. Tell us straight up: "I'm not just looking for a mate for myself; I'm trying to form a union with a man who will be willing to be the head of this family." You know what a declaration such as that is? That, sweetheart, is a requirement. You've told him in a nice, not-so-subtle-but-sweet way that the only way a man is going to be a part of your life is if he agrees to be a part of your children's lives, too. A real man is going to be okay with that because you've told him that if he's going to be a part of your life, you and the kids are a package deal, and that he will get dismissed quickly if you feel like he's not right for or good to the kids. With that information, with your requirements so clearly laid out, he's going to either run for the hills, or try to figure out how to make this thing work. Go ahead, invite him to come with you and the kids to the zoo, or invite him over to your mom's house for a family barbecue. See what he says—what he does. If he says, "Nah, I ain't going over there, I got to watch *Monday Night Football*," and it's Saturday, then guess what? He's probably not the one for you. Usually, how a relationship starts is a good sign of how it's going to end up, and if a man starts out not interested in your family, what makes you think that after you sleep with him, he's going to suddenly develop an affection for your family? But if he brings a game of Scrabble or Monopoly over to the house and sits down on the floor and plays for an hour or he invites you and your family to join him on an outing, then he just might be a keeper.

For those of you who are thinking strictly from a safety standpoint, please know that I'm not telling you to bring a man you hardly know into your house and leave him sitting there with your kids, unsupervised. Of course, when someone you're just getting to know is in your home near your kids, you're going to sit there the whole time, watching. What's he going to do—touch your daughter on the thigh while you're sitting on the couch right next to her? Or put your son in a choke hold at the dinner table? Be realistic: no man is going to walk in your house and abuse anyone with you sitting nearby. And if you're *that* concerned about bringing a man into your house, you can always go to a public place—somewhere where plenty of people will be able to eyeball what's going on and give a detailed accounting to the authorities if he steps out of line and you have to chop him in the neck.

For those of you who are dating men with children, don't expect him to introduce the kids early, necessarily, because wherever his child is, most likely his child's mother isn't too far away. And the last thing he needs or wants is for his kid to run back to his ex talking about the "nice lady" Daddy had over to the house; next thing you know, his ex is laying down the new custody terms, which do not include having her baby around any strange woman she hasn't previously ran a background check on and authorized, especially if that woman is trying to lay up in her ex's house. So a man with children from a previous relationship recognizes he needs to ration out the female encounters with his kids if he wants to try to keep a modicum of peace with his ex and actually see his kids again. If you're not somebody he's trying to have around for any amount of time, he's not going to waste his "girl-encounter ration" on you, knowing that you're not worth the grief he's going to suffer when his children go back and tell their mommy he had a woman in the house. He's decided in his mind you're not worth it.

If he asks you to meet the kids, thereby using one of his girl-encounter rations, be sure of this: he's decided you're worth the pain he'll have to suffer when the ex hears about it.

How will he let you know which category you fit in? If after, say, your fifth date he's still telling you, "By the way, we have to go out on Sunday because this Saturday is my time with the kids and it's the only time I have with them, so . . ." then he doesn't want you around them—he's telling you you're not worth the potential headache. But if he says something like "I got the kids this Saturday, how about we go to the beach or the park?" then he's thinking he can figure out how to deal with the ex later—right now, he wants nothing more than to be with you and the kids.

Want to smoke out whether he's got "good father" potential or not? The following list isn't foolproof, but it will certainly give you some food for thought about the things you should be taking into account as you consider whether this man is right for your kids—or if you should take the kids and run in the other direction.

YOU KNOW HE'LL MAKE A GOOD FATHER IF. . .

1. He tells you he likes kids, and actually would like to have one someday.

2. He expresses interest in meeting your children.

3. He shows up to the house with gifts—for the kids. (Of course, if he brings an Xbox for Mikey and disappears for a few hours, then that might be a problem.)

4. He lets the children see that he sincerely respects and likes (and even loves) their mother.

5. He makes a kid-friendly date with you and invites your children along.

6. He takes you and the kids to church.

7. He has a good job and a solid work history.

8. He's kind to his mother and checks in with her often (but mama's boys need not apply).

9. His nieces and nephews spend considerable time with him.

10. He has younger siblings he helped care for when he was younger—and they made it through, unscathed.

11. He has a pet, and it actually gets fed and taken care of.

12. He keeps his house clean and knows how to cook a few decent meals.

13. He's financially prepared to care for you and your children, or he has the desire to.

14. He can and is willing to comfort your child when she hurts herself. (If he starts hyperventilating at the sight of blood, this might be a situation—especially if he's already told you he's a doctor.)

15. He doesn't faint at the sight of diapers.

16. He can get down and dirty with your children—squirting them with a water hose, shooting hoops at the park, getting buried in the sand at the beach—and like it. (Though you don't want him to get *too* excited about playing "Tea Party" with the dolls.)

17. He doesn't lose his mind when someone spills food and drinks in his car, or puts a muddy footprint on the back of his seat—it shows he's not so fussy about messy kids (because nothing wrecks your car quicker than having kids; his seats *will* see the inside of a Happy Meal).

18. He can make it through a one-on-one game with your child and maybe even let him win once (Note: dunking on an eight-year-old and yelling, "In your face!" is not something a good potential father would do).

19. He's willing and able to teach you how to play a sport—which shows he has the patience of Job.

20. He's willing to go to family functions with you and the kids—even after hearing the stories about your crazy aunt Thelma and how she likes to get a little tipsy and call out your new boyfriends in front of company.

21. He's actually interested in how your child is doing in school, and not only encourages him to do well, but gives suggestions on how he can excel.

22. He can be gentle with your kids, but he's capable of being firm with them, too (though you don't want to see him start taking off his belt within the first half hour of meeting the children; I know kids can be bad, but that's a little much).

23. He's capable of forgiveness, and shows that, even when your kid does the seemingly unforgivable—or at least the highly questionable.

13

STRONG, INDEPENDENT—
AND LONELY—
WOMEN

A world without women would go a little something like this:

Men wouldn't wash or shave.

We wouldn't work.

Our wardrobe would be pretty simple: sweats, T-shirts, and socks—maybe some sneakers if we absolutely had to go outside.

There'd definitely be no need for dishes or vegetables or much food for that matter—a paper plate or two, some cold cuts, pizza, and beer would do just fine.

Furniture in the house would be kept to a minimum: we'd

have a recliner, a refrigerator, a really big television, and, of course, a remote.

We'd need only two television channels: ESPN and ESPN2.

And we wouldn't need to go on vacation—we'd just go to Vegas. They've got everything we need in Vegas—you can gamble there, smoke cigars, eat steak, play golf, and go to the strip club, and really, you wouldn't need that "what happens in Vegas stays in Vegas" slogan because men wouldn't go blabbing about what they did, anyway.

This is all to say that men are very simple creatures who would be prone to doing some very simple things if not for the women in our lives. After all, you all are the masters of "handling it": you work full-time, then come home to the full-time job of being wives and mothers and everything to everybody; you're raising kids (all too many of you without any help from the men who helped create them); you're making most of the major purchasing decisions in our households; you're taking over key positions in the corporate world and bringing home the bacon (some of you more than the men in your lives); you're excelling in college, where you outnumber young men at a ridiculous rate; and you're holding up our churches and educating our children in the school system, in effect, nurturing and protecting our minds and spirits. We men welcome and appreciate this more than you ever will know (mainly because we're a little too proud sometimes to 'fess up to it).

Still, the strength it takes to "handle it" is not, in a man's mind, where a woman's power lies. To us, your power comes from one simple thing: you're a woman, and we men will do anything humanly possible to impress you so that, ultimately, we can be with you. You're the driving force behind why we wake up every day. Men go out and get jobs and hustle to make money because of women. We drive fancy cars because of women. We dress nice, put on cologne, get haircuts and try to look all shiny and new for you. We do all of this because the more our game is stepped up, the more of you we get.

You're the ultimate prize to us.

This may be a hard pill for you to swallow and some of you may be offended by what I'm about to say, but I say this in truth and an abiding love for the opposite sex: somewhere along the way, women lost sight of this. Maybe in part because we men have played so many games, pulled so many tricks out of our hats—just plain done so much wrong in our quest to get women—that we've convinced you all that you are not important to us. Perhaps it has to do with how women are raised these days—there's been the constant encouragement from your mothers and aunties and grandmas and female mentors to educate yourselves and get great jobs and to be independent women, no matter the cost, even if it means putting off having serious relationships. Or maybe you all have just been worn down by the constant media obsession with perfection, with everything from magazine covers to television shows, to commercials, and blogs, and everything else telling you to nip it and tuck it and suck it in and dress it up and look like Halle Berry and Beyoncé if you want to attract a good man, knowing full well that all of you possess a great beauty all your own, and only Halle can look like Halle, and only Beyoncé can look like Beyoncé.

Whatever the case, we men are no longer connecting with that special part of you that makes you a woman—that thing that makes you so very beautiful to us, and that also happens to make us feel more like men. As I've already explained, the three ways a man shows you he loves you is by professing, providing, and protecting. Which means that if you've got your own money, your own car, your own house, a Brinks alarm system, a pistol, and a guard dog, and you're practically shouting from the rooftops that you don't need a man to provide for you or protect you, then we will see no need to keep coming around. What in the world do you need us for if you have all of that?

Don't misunderstand what I'm saying here. We don't mind it if you have yourself totally together—you can have your own house, you can have your own money, you can own your own car. You can have the Brinks alarm system, the guard dog, and the pistol, too. But if the man who is pursuing your affection is never allowed by you to exhibit his ability to provide or protect, then how can he possibly see himself professing his love to a woman who has not allowed him to feel like a man? The things you've acquired and gained financially and educationally can never be bigger than the relationship with the man. His DNA will not allow for that. Translation: we appreciate it when women treat us like men, when you let us know that you *need* us. The need to feel needed is way bigger to us than we've let on; we have to feel needed by you in order to fulfill our destiny as a man.

Of course, I've heard women say, "I'm not going to belittle myself to make him feel more like a man—if he can't handle my money and my success and my independence, then he can't handle me!" We understand and can handle strong women. In fact, we're the products of strong women—women who "handle it." It's no secret that you allow us men to believe we're the head of the household, but it's you who makes all the key decisions in the house and with the kids. It's no secret to us that no matter who's bringing in the most money, it's you who ultimately handles the finances and allocates how the cash is going to be spent. It's no secret that when we argue, we may act like we're right, but we know that ultimately, if we want to restore the peace, you're going to get your way. We're cool with all of this. But if you say things to this effect without keeping up the charade of our being essential to the household or you handle our egos with anything less than great care—then we're not going to want to be involved with you. In our minds, if you've got your own money, you don't need ours. If you know karate and can knock somebody flat on his behind by yourself, then you don't need our protection. And if we can't exercise two of the major components that make up who we are as men—providing and protecting—then we're not about to profess our love for you. We absolutely will not say, "I'm your man" if you don't let us fulfill who we are. What *will* end up happening instead? We'll sleep with you and then walk away.

It's the hard truth, but that's real.

When I was a young man, I was in a relationship with a woman who I thought I loved. I had dropped out of college and was in between jobs, just starting to find my way as a comedian. She was an enormous help to me; I was struggling, and she was holding it down for us financially, I admit, but I thought I was more than making up for my lack of cash by being all I could be around the house—doing what was necessary to keep our home in order. See, that's what being in a real relationship is all about—finding that balance, even in the midst of adversity. And adversity *will* come. Those wedding vows they make you say? The preacher makes you say them because he and everyone else who's ever been married knows what's coming. For better or for worse? Worse is coming. In sickness and in health? Somebody is going to get sick. For richer or for poorer? Somebody might end up broke, temporarily laid off. Hard times will certainly come. The question is, how are you going to deal with it?

This was made clear to a friend of mine one particular day when he went grocery shopping. His woman was loading up the cart with everything she needed for the house—the meats, the vegetables, the fruits, the drinks, and everything. And then they turned down the aisle with the pineapple juice. Now one thing you need to know about my friend—he loves pineapple juice. Steak with pineapple juice—I can't tell you which is better to him. And when they turned down that aisle, the first thing he put his hand on during that entire grocery store trip was a bottle of pineapple juice. He didn't think anything of it— just grabbed a bottle and dropped it into the cart. She had her back turned when he did it, but when she turned around and saw the pineapple juice in there on the pile of groceries, she snatched it out and said, "What is this?"

"Pineapple juice," he said simply.

"And who put this pineapple juice in the basket?" she asked.

"Well, I did," he said, a little confused. Who else in the world would have put a bottle of pineapple juice into their cart?

"You," she practically spit, "don't have any money."

And then she did the unthinkable: she took that bottle of pineapple juice and purposely dropped it on the floor; it hit the tile with the loudest crash, and broke into what looked like a million little pieces of shiny glass shards and yellow liquid—all of it just inches away from their feet. She glanced at it, then gave him the eye, and pushed the grocery cart on—away from the mess and him.

He walked out the store and waited for her; when she finally came out, he loaded the groceries into the car with tears in his eyes. You just can't imagine how that hurt him. He knew he didn't have any money, but all he wanted was a damn bottle of pineapple juice, and in that singular act, in that one moment, his lady shoved into his face that she didn't consider him to be a man. It was more important to her in that moment to prove what he already knew—that he wasn't fulfilling his role as a provider. I'm not suggesting that she didn't have the right to have a man who was pulling his weight. But if she knew him—and men—she would have understood that making him feel less than a man wasn't going to get her what she needed and wanted out of her man. Her actions were only going to drive him away.

Not long after, he left her.

And that is pretty much the reaction you can expect from men in similar situations where a woman makes more than her partner and she rubs that fact in his face. Will he be intimidated by your money and your success? Of course. Because you're taking him out of his role as a man—to be the provider. It's what society expects of him, and really, what you've been taught to expect of men, too—that he be able to sweep you up and take care of you. Sure, when a man is young and doesn't know any better, he's busy being all this other stuff he thinks fits into what it means to be a man: dating an excess of women; recklessly spending his money on things he doesn't really need, much less can afford; using his muscle instead of his brain in his quest to appear tough. But most of us grow out of this eventually, and when we do, we recognize that a real man provides for the ones he loves. Even a male convict will sit behind bars and tell you, "The first thing I'm going to do when I get out of here is take care of my family and get a job—that's all I want to do." Most every man comes to that realization. Some men never come out of the ignorance and die fools—alone. But for the most part, when we get around other men and try to validate our manhood, it's not about how many women we've got, but who we're taking care of.

We are trained to be providers for you, and you are trained to look for that in us. So the moment that order of things is thrown off, the relationship is out of sync. If a woman also has the bad habit of throwing a man's deficiencies in his face, then he has a problem of a whole different magnitude. He's going to struggle with not being the provider and she's going to feel like his ego is getting in the way of her happiness. And everyone involved is bound to get—and be—miserable.

So how do we get through this situation?

Don't give up your money, or your job, or your education, or the pride and dignity that come with all of that.

Just be a lady.

Oh, I can hear the collective teeth sucking—it's as loud as a police siren and helicopter whir in Compton—I can see the universal arm folding and eyebrow raising as well. But your getting hot and bothered by what I'm saying isn't going to change the fact that men, no matter what their financial situation, background, social status, or backstory, want their women to let them take care of them. And I say to you defiant ones, go ahead and act like this isn't important if you want to, but the women who accept that it's okay to let the guy take the lead sometime are going to win. So do you want a man or not?

You can do this.

We know you're strong enough to move the television set. But you should let him do it; say it's too heavy for you—it's a man's job.

Yes, you're right—there's nothing wrong with your arm and you are perfectly capable of opening your own car door. But doggone it, when you're going somewhere with a man, let him treat you like a lady and open the car door for you. If he doesn't automatically open said car door, stand by the darn thing and don't get in the vehicle until he realizes he needs to get his behind out of the driver's seat and come around and open the car door for you. That's his job.

We get that you've got plenty of money to pay for dinner. But sit there and let him pick up that check. That's what he's supposed to do when he's out with a woman on a date.

Yes, you are independent and you don't need anyone to take out the trash for you or hang your pictures or run to the Home Depot and pick up the supplies you need to fix the sink. But I lie to you not: if you put your finger in your mouth and act like you haven't a clue what to do or the strength to do it, your man will step right in and handle that for you—with a smile if you add a hearty, "Baby, thank you so much for doing this for me—I don't know what I'd do without you."

See, a lot of men would be better men if they were required to be, well, men. We're in this new age, and women have taken on these roles out of necessity—I'll admit that. But at some point, you're either going to have to accept that you're going to be the big ol' strong, lonely woman, or you're going to have to back down and just be a lady. Women play roles all the time—why is it when it comes to this, you're so unwilling to play the role, even when you know it's going to give you what you want and need? In the long run, being a girl allows you to relax. Why not take the opportunity to relax? Honest to goodness, I promise you it's not hard, it won't kill you, and whatever it is that you need, he will hop to it if you just show him a little appreciation.

Take a page from my wife and I: there's not a day that goes by that we don't compliment each other at least several times a day, but on one specific day recently, when she left me in charge of the kids while she ran some errands and did some work around the house, she saw I was worn out from chasing behind the children. Chasing behind children is not something I do. I mean I can do it but it's exhausting. Come on. Still, when Marjorie walked into the room and saw the harried look on my face, she very sweetly flipped the script on me and said, "Steve, thank you so much for watching the children—you're a great father." Boy, I can't tell you how good that made me feel. She had hardly gotten the words out of her mouth before I hopped to, making sure those kids kept out of her way and stayed quiet while she was finishing up what she had to do. Had that compliment not come through, I would have been salty about having to sit around with the kids all day when there were so many other things that I could have been doing—and wanted to do. That compliment, you see, made me remember why I was in the game, and especially why Marjorie is on the team.

Appreciating a man, not undermining his confidence, is the best way to get the best out of your guy. And the best way to appreciate him is by being a girl, and especially letting him be a man.

Now, I'm convinced that being a girl is a lost art form—something that every woman can use some lessons in. So I've taken the liberty of showing you how to be a girl in some of the basic but most important situations in which you'll find yourself with a man. Guaranteed, if he's worth his salt, he'll be all in.

HOW TO BE A GIRL ON A DATE

Don't tell him where you'd like to go—tell him the kind of food and atmosphere you enjoy, and then let him figure out a place that he thinks will suit your taste.

Don't tell him you'll drive—let him get you to where you all need to go.

Don't tell him you want to go dutch—let him pay.

Don't invite him up for a nightcap—kiss him good night and let him figure out what he needs to do to *earn* the cookie (but not before the ninety-day probation ends).

HOW TO BE A GIRL AROUND THE HOUSE

Don't try to fix the sink, the car, the toilet, or anything else—let him do it.

Don't take out the garbage, paint, or mow the lawn—that's his job.

Don't do any of the heavy lifting—he was born with the muscle it takes to move sofas/television sets/bookshelves and the like.

Don't be afraid to make a meal or two—the kitchen is both your and his friend.

Don't wear a T-shirt to bed every night—a little lingerie never hurt anybody.

14

HOW TO GET THE RING

Your man knows what you want: the ultimate commitment—The Ring.

He knows, too, what he needs: you.

It seems obvious, then, that he would get himself to the jeweler, pick out a nice, hefty diamond, and then plot out an on-bended-knee proposal that would make the "will you marry me?" pitch that Grammy award–winning singer Seal made to supermodel Heidi Klum—he proposed in an igloo he had built on top of a glacier fourteen thousand feet above sea level—look like an invitation to the prom.

But your proposal never comes.

And the way your man is acting, it's not coming anytime soon.

And so, you wait. And wait. And wait some more.

This is the story of all-too-many women—girlfriends who are putting in some serious work not only because they love their men, but because they want to prove they're The One. Everybody is clear about how you prove to him you're The One: Do all the things for him a wife would do—support him emotionally, be loyal, work it out in the bedroom, tell him you love him often and show it, too. Maybe live with him. Have his babies. Get close—really close—to his mom and sisters and friends. Basically, you give him everything he needs and all of what he wants.

Check out this "Strawberry Letter" from a listener who called herself "Biological Clock Ticker," a thirty-one-year-old single, childless woman in a relationship she said feels like a "three-year-long booty call":

> He tells me he loves me and wants me to have his chil-
> dren. My biological clock is ticking like crazy, and we
> have been trying for the past year to get pregnant, to
> no avail (I believe that this is a sign). The problem is
> that he says he does not want to be in a committed re-
> lationship or marriage because he doesn't want to
> answer to anyone. As long as I have known him, I have
> shown him that I am not at all like the other women
> that he has dated. I was there for him when he injured
> himself, quit his job, when his father died, and when
> he was unemployed for months. I have been encourag-
> ing him, and am there for him financially and physi-

cally. I've been waiting and hanging in there, hoping
he'll marry me because I don't think that I will get
anyone else that would want to have a child with me.
Am I being a fool for waiting for him? Should I just let
it go?

She and all too many women in similar predicaments can't
understand why, after all of this hard work, he won't give her
the one thing she needs and wants. Well, let me break it down
for her and you. Your man hasn't asked you to marry him because of one or more of the following reasons: (1) he is still
married to someone else; (2) you're really not the one he wants;
or, the real answer you don't want to hear, (3) you haven't required him to marry you or set a date.

In fact, I know of a few guys whose ladies are smack-dab in
the middle of this predicament right now. One that stands out
is a couple that dated for a year before she ended up pregnant.
To her credit, the single mom (she has a son from an earlier
failed relationship) knew she didn't want to have a second child
with a man who wasn't there to help raise her kids, so she made
it simple for him: "I'm only going to have this child if you're
willing to be a father for real—not this part-time/every-once-
in-a-while/when-I-feel-like-it kind of dad." And, faced with
the prospect of losing her and his baby, he stepped up to the
plate: He agreed to be there for their child, and gave up his
apartment, and moved in with his girlfriend while they prepared for the birth of their son.

Oh, she thought the proposal, the ring, and the wedding would follow shortly after the baby was born. To his credit, her boyfriend did come through with a ring. But she's been wearing it for *seven* years now, and though she's been hoping, waiting, and praying for a wedding date, they're no closer to walking down the aisle today than they were the day their child was born. They share a home. They share parenting responsibilities. They share bills, schedules, car notes, church pews, and most certainly a bed. But they don't share the last name or a marriage certificate.

She can't understand why they're *playing house* instead of making an *official home* together. He feels as if they've got a home, and really, there's not much more need to go any further than they already have.

And this is the dilemma.

See, to some men, marriage fits into the same category as eating vegetables: you know it's something you should be doing, but you don't really want to because, well, the greasy, fat-filled, salty, juicy burger and fries is just so much more satisfying. I've told you time and again in this book that we men are very simple creatures, and if it were not for women, we'd be living rather, well, simply—the money would go to mostly shiny things, our time would be spent watching sports and strippers, and there would be no need for most of us to keep a clean house or dress nice or do anything other than play video games. We're happy living this way—it makes us feel young and carefree. Marriage does not. Responsibility and marriage do not fit into that feeling, until all of the playing gets tired and we realize we have to be grown-ups, or something—or someone—makes us grow up.

But here's what you need to know: men are pretty clear that marriage is what women want—that despite your independence, despite the statistics that say half the marriages in America end in divorce, despite the amount of time, work, sweat, and tears you know you'll have to pour into building an imperfect relationship, in the end, you women still believe in the fairy tale of the husband and the house and the white picket fence and the 2.5 kids.

Men are also clear that they can slowly give out the things that make it seem like they're making the march to the altar—just to keep you hanging in there. Trust me when I say this: men do everything with a purpose, and in the case where a man dates you for an extended length of time, or moves in with you, or gives you a ring, but still refuses to be pinned down on setting a wedding date? He's doing it to lock you down. He wants you, and he doesn't want anyone else to have you.

And I'm here to tell you, the only reason a man gets away with a lengthy engagement or holds off the proposal altogether is because his woman hasn't *required* him to set the date; she is stupidly sitting there allowing her boyfriend to dictate to her when he's ready, though she slept with this man, cut off any other prospective husbands, and, in some cases, moved in with him and even had his children.

I simply can't be diplomatic here.

It's just plain dumb.

Get into your man's mind-set here: if a man is willing to be your boyfriend at length, live with you, be an involved father, or give you a ring, he has already taken himself off the player's list—technically, he's scratched his name off the sport fishing registry. He can't bring babes to the house. He can't talk on the phone or take any phone calls from babes at the house. He can't leave to go see a babe when he wants to—or stay with her all night. He knows he can't give his money to any other woman because he's pooling it with you. Why does a man in a committed relationship with you accept the above list of "he can'ts"?

Because he wants you and he doesn't want to lose you.

So now there's only one more step to get the marriage equation: the setting of the wedding date. You know you want it, so here's what you do: get some requirements and standards and enforce them—tell him, "I love you, you love me, we're in a terrific relationship—one that I've always dreamed about. And what I want now is to be married to you. So I need you to set a date, and get back to me in a couple of weeks. If I don't get asked by then, then please know I'm not sitting around waiting for you to dictate when my happiness button gets pushed. The arrangements we have now are not making me happy."

What? This is a perfectly reasonable request. Otherwise, how long are you going to stay in the arrangement where you're not getting what you want—four years? Ten years? Forever?

The timeline is yours; stop giving up your power. The

moment we see you're willing to put aside your hopes of walking down the aisle, we're going to shelve it, too. And we're going to go on ahead and keep on renting you out, with the *option* to buy if you let us. Don't be the Baltic Avenue on the Monopoly board game—the one that anyone can just roll the dice, land on, and pay a couple of dollars to chill on without any obligations or worries. You've got to go to Broadway on the game board; make your man round the corner and land on that high end property—recognize that you're prime real estate that's for purchase only.

Note: This is *not* about asking your man to marry you. It's about taking yourself out of that 1945 mentality, where you stand around waiting for some guy to beg you for your hand in marriage. You've had it drummed into your head so cold—that "I'll never ask a man to marry me" thing—that you've lost all sensibility when it comes to getting what *you* want. But it's not 1945 anymore! Back in the day when my parents and their generation were courting and getting married, women could afford to wait around for the man to get it together because really, the options for men were limited. If a guy lived in a farmhouse, the next farmhouse was two miles away, and that one might not have a girl in it—just two more boys—so he'd have to walk another two miles to actually see a potential mate, much less find *the* one. And when they courted, they *courted*; he had to walk over there, write little messages on rocks on the way over so everybody knew his intentions, leave a note by the tree and send up smoke signals so the girl knew what was up. Oh, the courtship was far more romantic, because the men knew they had to behave properly—not just for their intendeds, but their intendeds' daddies. The boys had to go over to the house, ask permission to sit in the room together, and the adults were present because there weren't any extra rooms for them to sit in alone. And that courting culminated in the men pulling the fathers aside and, with their shoulders squared and chins up, asking the fathers for their daughters' hands in marriage. And whatever the father said is what went.

Now women have been taught all their lives that if a man loves you, he will court you and ask for your hand in marriage. The problem with this is that you've been trained to use twentieth-century logic in twenty-first-century situations. There's no slim pickings of women out here—women are at every turn, working with men, living in apartment buildings with them, riding the bus and trains with them, hanging out at the clubs with them. Technology's such that you can contact a woman without ever even seeing her. It's not 1945 anymore—you can't hang on to those old ways. This, "If he wants to marry me, he'll ask me" thing has got to stop. Because we're not going to ask you when you're ready—we're going to play with you until you give us your requirements and standards, and stand by them. I'm not telling you to get on bended knee. I'm telling you to set a timeline for the ring and the date, and tell the man you want to be married to what it is.

I recognize that this is hard. But let me tell you what's really hard: dating/living with/having a baby with a man who has no intention of marrying you and eight years up the road, he walks out and you're left to find a new man/pay all the bills after years of splitting them with someone else/raising those kids on your own. Oh, it can be done. But recognize just how hard that will be. All I'm suggesting is that you get the little uncomfortable moments out of the way early—let him know now what you want and expect. Make clear to him what you're worth, and that you come at a cost; tell him how much you're worth like you're about to list yourself on eBay for a million dollars. Break down your value: say, "I respect you, I adore you, I'm affectionate, I pay attention to you, I'm punctual, I'm kind, I'm loyal, I'll have your children and love them madly—and all of this is available for a handsome sum. I need *your* time, loyalty, support, affection, attention, punctuality, kindness, gentleman ways—I need the doors opened, chairs pulled out, your respect, and above all else, your love. I also expect a diamond ring and a walk down the aisle."

Now when a man hears this, he's going to pay attention, because you've placed a high value on yourself. He'll see that and question the situation: "Is she worth all of that?" If your cost is too high, he will move on. But you don't want that guy anyway, right? He's just looking to rent you. People who rent don't care anything about the property they're with—they let it get run down, beat up, don't care what it looks like. They use the space, and when they find something better, they decline the new lease and they move on out and on to the next rental.

You want the guy who is ready to make the Broadway purchase—the one who's looking to move in, stay awhile, take care of the lawn, make sure the plumbing is right, paint the walls, add furniture, pay the mortgage faithfully. You know, make your house a home. That guy right there? He's the one who will take responsibility and pop the question, like you need him to.

After all, boys shack. Men build homes.

Demand that he be a man about it. If he's not in love with you, he's not going to go for any of this, so now you know. But if he loves you, he will profess it, he will provide for you, and he will protect you. If he really loves you, the ultimate profession is, "This is my wife." You can start with, "This is my girl," or "This is my baby's mother," or even, "This is my fiancée." But after a couple of years, you need to move beyond this fiancée title. At the very least, you deserve clarity. Because women do not do well without clarity. The thing you all want to know is: Where's this relationship going? Do you love me? Am I the one? What do you see for us?

That's it in a nutshell—every man knows this is coming up the road for him. He may not be ready for it now, but if he's not ready for it now and you are, then you don't have a good match, do you? So why waste all of your valuable years on something that's not going where you want it to go? Instead, you should seek out someone else who wants to go where you're going. I truly believe that's why there are so many women in their midthirties unmarried—because somewhere along the line, they just didn't put their foot down and move on. But I can tell you from personal experience: put your foot down, set some standards, and watch how fast he falls in line. The reason I'm married to Marjorie today is because she had a timeline, some requirements, and some standards. I saw them early in our relationship; I saw them on the night our relationship was about to end; I saw them when I got her back. I'll tell you this much, if I still had the factory job at Ford and she needed $400 of my $600 paycheck, I would have given it to her.

I want to protect her.

And she makes me proud to be her man.

You can have this, too. Don't be another heartbreak story. Start putting yourself first—get where you want to be, and make your man be all that he can be. Remember this: the number one cause of failure in this country is the *fear* of failure. Fear paralyzes you from taking action. Don't be afraid to lose him, because if a man truly loves you, he's not going anywhere.

15

QUICK ANSWERS TO THE
QUESTIONS YOU'VE ALWAYS
WANTED TO ASK

If I've told you once, I've told you a million times: men are really simple creatures. And there are some subjects we're just not going to spend a whole lot of time thinking about—we're just going to answer your questions, straight, no chaser. So I asked a bunch of my female co-workers and associates to fire some questions at me—things they've always wanted to know that their girlfriends just couldn't answer for them in a satisfying way. They asked—I answered. Here it goes:

WHAT DO MEN FIND SEXY?

SH: Men have different aesthetics, so what might be a turnoff for one man may be a total turn-on for another. Rest assured, though, that no matter the flaws you find when you look at yourself in the mirror, somewhere on God's earth, you are really "doing it" for someone—someone out there is attracted to you exactly the way you are. A confident woman is incredibly attractive, no matter what mold she fits in. Men are also very visual people, so there is no question men will check out a woman's clothes, the way she walks, her makeup, her feet, her hands, her daintiness—little escapes our notice.

HOW DO MEN FEEL ABOUT PLASTIC SURGERY, WEAVES, COLORED CONTACTS, FAKE NAILS, ET CETERA?

SH: For the average man, whatever you're doing to make yourself look beautiful while you're hanging on his arm is cool by him. Boob jobs, tummy tucks, breast reductions, nose jobs—if it makes you feel beautiful, we're good. But if you're telling your man you want a nose job and he sees nothing wrong with the nose you already have, then maybe you ought to think about leaving your nose alone. Why run the risk of something going wrong when your man is already happy with the way you look? Why lose the extra weight if your man is happy with you the way you are? Sure, it's fine for you to do it if it's something you want to do for yourself. But a man isn't going to care about it one way or the other if he's already happy with what you have.

HOW DO MEN FEEL ABOUT DATING WOMEN WHO ARE SIGNIFICANTLY YOUNGER THAN THEM?

SH: A lot of men in their forties and fifties start trying to validate themselves by going out with women who are significantly younger. It's the equivalent of those same-age men going out and buying itty-bitty sports cars with big engines that make a lot of noise; they do this because their "engine" doesn't make a lot of noise anymore. This is especially true if that man doesn't have his life together. This isn't a reflection on women at all; it's his problem. But guess what? There's a younger man looking at you right now, saying to himself, "Wow—I sure wouldn't mind validating myself with her!" There's a lot of that going on, too, you know. Like I said before, there's somebody for everybody.

DO MEN PREFER SKINNY OR THICK WOMEN?

SH: Men like all kinds of women. There's a man out there for every body type. There are men who like them big, there are men who like only small, petite women, and there are men who prefer women who fit between those sizes. It runs the gamut. It does not matter what size you are—there is a man somewhere for you.

WILL YOU DATE OR MARRY A WOMAN WHO SMOKES?

SH: I wouldn't, and most nonsmokers wouldn't, either. The skin of women who smoke ages prematurely and their lips are stained. It ages them internally, too. And for me, it exhibits a weakness and a lack of understanding about their own health. Once we non-smoking men see that a woman doesn't care about her own health, we immediately equate that to her inability to care for her man and her kids. Most non-smoking men will not tolerate a smoking woman—not on a permanent basis. We'll sleep with you, but we're not taking you home.

WHAT DO MEN THINK OF THEIR WOMEN WHEN THEY GAIN WEIGHT, OR LOOK DIFFERENT THAN THEY DID IN THE BEGINNING OF THE RELATIONSHIP?

SH: A man who loves you is going to love you regardless. As we ourselves get bellies and love handles, we certainly understand yours. We get that you're not going to look exactly like you did when we first met you. If you can keep it in some kind of parameter, though— gain ten pounds, but avoid gaining a hundred—and be sexy and fix it up and look nice with whatever extra weight you've put on or taken off, we're cool. If your man is shallow, he'll insist he just can't see past it. But if a man recognizes that, a few pounds notwithstanding, you're still making an effort to do what it takes to be visually appealing, he will be fine with it.

DO MEN PREFER WOMEN IN FLATS OR HEELS?

SH: Heels, baby. Heels. If we could get athletic shoes with heels for women, we would. It's just a really sexy thing to us. I don't know a single man who prefers women in flats; I've never run into one. We all think heels make your legs more beautiful, they make your walk more feminine—and you, too. And that's what we're attracted to.

WOULD A MAN DATE A DUMB WOMAN?

SH: A smart man can't date a dumb woman. But he can *use* a dumb woman. Most smart men don't want to date a dumb woman because we need to know that she can handle herself and our affairs, especially if we're thinking about giving her a ring. She can't walk into the office party acting like the office dummy. Now, we don't mind having a woman on the side who is dumb and fine, but we won't keep her.

WHAT DO MEN THINK OF WOMEN WHO BUY MEN DRINKS?

SH: It's a total come-on. In our mind, if you want to buy us a drink, you want us. And if we think you want us, well, then, game on—we're coming in for the kill.

HOW DO MEN FEEL ABOUT WOMEN WHO DRINK?

SH: Some men like it, but a man who doesn't drink certainly isn't going to care for a woman who partakes in the spirits. Know, though, that no man likes a drunk woman, unless you're in college and we're heading back to your dorm room. Remember, men want women to act like ladies at all times. If you drink socially, cool. But if your man has to carry you out, because you've passed out, you're hanging on to someone else, or you're talking loud and telling him you like slamming down shots, it's going to be a problem.

SHOULD A WOMAN BUY A MAN GIFTS WHILE THEY'RE DATING?

SH: Only if you're in a committed relationship. Other than that, all he'll think is (a) you're trying to trap him, and (b) you expect something in return. Just wait and see what he's going to bring to your table first—let him be the man and spoil you. Real men like to do this for the women they care about. Note: Be thankful for the gifts he gives you, but don't take it as the end all/be all sign that you're going to get a ring next week. A gift is just that—a gift. Not a sign of things to come. Only his actions—the way he professes, protects, and provides for you—will give you a true sign of how this man feels about you.

HOW DO MEN FEEL ABOUT WOMEN WHO ASK FOR MONEY?

SH: Don't do it in the beginning of the relationship, unless you're perfectly comfortable with the title gold digger. But if you're in a relationship—just you and him—and you're really in a financial pinch, mention it and see how he reacts. Say, "I'm really in a crunch, and I'm embarrassed to ask, but I really need your help. Do you think you could loan me $100 to meet this payment? I'll pay you back as soon as I can." Most men who really care about you won't think anything of it if they have it.

WOULD MEN HELP THEIR WOMAN BUILD HER BUSINESS?

SH: Without a doubt. If you're dealing with a man whose life isn't on track, who isn't at peace with who he is, how much he makes, and what he does, you might have a guy who'd be reluctant to help because he's still struggling to reach his goals and won't have time to help you with yours. But if he has his act together and he's really secure in his manhood, he'll help.

DO YOU MIND IF YOUR WOMAN DOESN'T WORK?

SH: Not at all. These days it's almost a necessity for both the husband and the wife to work to make ends meet. But if a man is in a position to provide everything his family needs, most men would not have a problem with his woman staying home.

HOW DO MEN REALLY FEEL ABOUT WOMEN DRIVERS?

SH: This is the twenty-first century, so most men don't have a problem with women drivers. But there are still some old-fashioned, chauvinist men who think women should leave the driving to the opposite sex. I don't know what cave they're living in. Matter of fact, I haven't met any of them yet.

DOES IT MATTER IF A WOMAN LIKES SPORTS?

SH: No. Some guys like that, but mostly what they like is enjoying the game in peace. If you're not into it, go find something else to do.

DO MEN LIKE SHOPPING?

SH: We'll go if you make us and it's the only way we can spend time with you. But it's not what we want to do. Think about it: the Men's Department is almost always on the first floor, by the door, and always one of the smaller sections in the store. There is no juniors department, no couture department, none of that. It's so we can get in and get out. You never walk in and see men rummaging through the sales racks and holding shirts up to their chests and openly asking if they'd look better in the blue or the green. We go in knowing exactly what we want, and come out with it. Rarely anything more. In and out: that's what we like about shopping. Getting in, and getting out.

HOW DO MEN FEEL ABOUT INTERRACIAL DATING?

SH: It depends on the man. But really, who cares these days? It's not the big stink that it used to be. Personally I don't care. Love comes in every color— and if a person finds love and that person is of a different race from him or her, it shouldn't matter because the two of them found love. And isn't that what counts the most? Women have to make sure, though, that that's what they're doing it for. If she's doing it for some kind of status, then that's a horrible reason to get married to someone from a different race. But if she's doing it for love, more power to her.

WHY DON'T MEN LIKE TO CUDDLE AFTER SEX?

SH: Because we're hot. We're exhausted. We put in a lot of work, we're sweaty and burning up and we just need you to hold on a minute before you come climbing over to the side of our bed talking about holding something.

HOW DO YOU LET A MAN KNOW THAT HE'S NOT SATISFYING YOU SEXUALLY?

SH: It's not a good idea to break that news at the kitchen table or on a long car ride. Nothing good can come from that. When you question our sexual abilities, we get really nervous and really self-conscious really quickly. I suggest you break the news while you're in the act. We're a little bit more open to it then. Say something like, "Oh, I like it when you do this," or

"That's nice, baby, now do it this way," and watch him go to work. We'll put our backs into it then, because it makes us feel like we're pleasing you instead of absorbing complaints. During the act, we're open to any and all suggestions, as long as we think we're getting it.

WHAT IF WE WANT MORE SEX AND WE'RE NOT GETTING IT?

SH: Whatever you do, don't open this conversation with the dreaded four words: "We need to talk." Our defenses immediately go up, warning signs start flashing before our eyes, and now we're pretty confident whatever good time we had planned is about to be ruined. Instead, try telling your man spontaneously something like, "I just can't get enough of you." That will make him know that the bar is up there—he'll be more than willing to jump over it because you've made him feel like you want him, instead of like there's something wrong.

HOW LONG IS TOO LONG TO HOLD OUT ON SEX IF WE'RE FIGHTING?

SH: One day is more than enough punishment for us if we're talking about some kind of argument. You're mad about something he said about the kids and you don't want to have sex tonight? Okay. But tomorrow, if you're still mad about the kids and he's tapping you on the shoulder and you're shaking off his hand, that's a problem. Men are not going to hang in for that too long. But we'll go without longer if we violated your trust in some kind of way and we need to gain back your respect and trust. We understand that much.

HOW CAN A WOMAN TELL IF HER MAN IS ON THE DOWN LOW?

SH: I haven't a clue—only gay men, or women who've dated men on the down low, can answer that question for you. I don't fall into either of those categories.

HOW DO MEN FEEL ABOUT OPEN RELATIONSHIPS?

SH: If a man goes along with an "open relationship" or he offers it, he's doing so because you are not in his long-term plans. He does not see a future with you. Both of you can stop all this "We wanted some spice in the relationship" talk. When a man loves you, he's not trying to share you with anybody—period. When you find that guy who's willing, I will show you the guy who's not in love with you. We're just not cut out that way.

DO MEN GET BOTHERED WHEN YOU ASK THEM ABOUT THEIR PAST?

SH: Yes—it makes us uncomfortable. We think you're trying to dig deep into our soul when you start trolling through our past and, possibly, passing judgment on it. Still, you have the right to know about a man's past. Just don't ask about it on the first date, because you will not get an honest answer, ever. He hasn't even decided about how permanent this thing between you is going to be—there'll be no need to reveal the soul. Don't even waste your time asking about his previous woman; all he's going to claim is hurt, not what he may have done to her. Give your relationship time, and he'll reveal what you need to know.

HOW DO YOU FEEL ABOUT A WOMAN WHO DOES NOT WANT YOUR LAST NAME AFTER MARRIAGE?

SH: Most men have a problem with that. Think about the three ways I told you a man shows his love. He protects, provides, and professes. And if we can't say "This is Mrs. Harvey," then you're taking away the very core of how we show our love. We also need to know that we have your loyalty, and you show that by taking our name. We really don't care how important your dad's name or your family name is to you; we're about to start a family. A man needs to know you're as committed to this family as you are to your old one. You can hyphenate it if you want to, but that last name really needs to be the same as your man's. And if you're not committed to that, then why don't you just go marry your daddy?

IS IT GOOD TO MAKE YOUR MAN JEALOUS SO HE KNOWS YOU CAN GET ANOTHER MAN IF YOU WANTED TO?

SH: There's no need to do that; we've got that covered. We're pretty clear that our woman can walk out at any time. But if you push it and try to make us jealous, you're going to be playing a dangerous game. Doing that almost always triggers a reflex in a man; he might be liable to say, "Oh, okay—two can play at that game!" If you feel like you have to make him jealous because you're not getting the attention you want, you might want to consult the "Men Need Standards—Get Some" chapter, and then use some of those tips to get the man you need and deserve.

ARE MEN OKAY WITH THEIR WOMEN HAVING MALE FRIENDS?

SH: I strongly suggest that if you're in a fully committed relationship, all the chitchat you're having with a male friend gets dialed back. Take down the college pictures of the two of you, don't let him call the house or send gifts and such; continuing this every day is just asking for trouble. Think about it: I don't care if you could only see her picture in the dark with an invisible blue light; if your man kept a picture of another woman in his personal belongings, you'd lose your mind. How would you like it if he had a woman calling the house asking to speak to him? Or he accepted flowers from her? Exactly. What I suggest is that you avoid doing anything that will make your man have uncomfortable thoughts about you and someone else—period. Form a two-handed circle and don't let anyone else in, especially male "friends." You'll be happy you did.

WHY DO SOME MEN HIT WOMEN?

SH: Mostly out of weakness and a need to control something in their lives. But I have found that men who hit women have no tales or stories of hitting men. They're *that* weak.

WHAT ABOUT GIRLFRIENDS—HOW DO YOU FEEL ABOUT THEM?

SH: We don't mind them. I mean, your man can't tell you not to have girlfriends any more than you can say he can't go play golf with the boys. Girlfriends are fine.

HOW DO MEN FEEL ABOUT GOSSIP?

SH: We hate gossiping. But we know we can't stop it. It's an invasion of privacy, and a man is pretty confident that if you and your friends are willing to talk about other people together, then your friends are probably talking about you and him, too. Keep that in mind the next time you start getting all into other people's business.

WILL MEN TALK ABOUT THEIR WOMEN TO OTHER MEN?

SH: Not if she's The One. Wives and significant others are off-limits in conversations between men, because no man wants you thinking about his woman any kind of way, much less in a romantic or sexual way. Every man is clear on this. However, if you're not The One—you're just someone that we're "doing" while we look for The One—then you will be talked about, rest assured.

IS GETTING ON HIS MOM'S SIDE IMPORTANT?

SH: Look, if you don't have a good relationship with his mother, and she doesn't care for you, it is going to be stressful. Any woman who has been in a relationship with a man for ninety days should have met the family already, and if he hasn't introduced you, then you either need to ask why, or you should pretty much accept that he's not interested in forging a long-term relationship with you. If you're good enough for him to make it to his bed, you should be good enough to meet his mother.

IF A MAN'S SISTER DOESN'T LIKE HIS GIRLFRIEND, WILL HE BREAK UP WITH HER?

SH: Hell, no. No man is breaking up with his girl because she doesn't get along with family members (other than his mother). A sister doesn't have to come around to the house and be a part of family functions if she can't get along with the woman a man loves. The same holds true for cousins, aunties, and uncles.

IF HE DOESN'T LIKE YOUR FAMILY, WILL HE STAY WITH YOU?

SH: If you put your family before him, he's out of there.

HOW DO MEN FEEL ABOUT THE BABY DADDY?

SH: It's cool—men know the child has a father, and if he's in his kid's life, we understand we'll have to have some type of interaction with him. But your new man needs to be able to come to your house and be himself. If he's in a committed relationship with you and he sees the kids doing something wrong and he can't say anything to them about it, then you're not letting him be the provider and protector he wants to be, and that's going to be a problem for him. You can't allow a man to buy school clothes, help put a roof over your head, put groceries in the refrigerator and buy gas for the car, and then tell him he doesn't have the right to be a father figure—if not a father—to the kids. If that's the case, then what is his point of being there? You'll have to figure out some kind of balance—one that allows your child's father to do his job, but also allows your new man to do his job, too. And if he can't participate in raising the child, that could explain why the baby's daddy left in the first place.

WILL MY MAN EXPECT ME TO BE FRIENDS WITH HIS CHILD'S MOTHER?

SH: Look, there are only a few Will and Jada Pinkett Smiths in this world. If you're one of them, congratulations. But really, he's not betting that you two will hit it off too well, and so he won't force the issue.

IS IT OKAY TO INTERRUPT HIS DAY AT WORK TO TALK?

SH: If you're calling to say, "I have a special surprise for you when you get home," that's a good interruption. But if it's a phone call to talk about petty problems? Not a good interruption. Just because you feel like saying something right now this minute doesn't mean it should be said.

WHAT'S THE INTERNATIONAL MAN SIGNAL FOR "I'M NO LONGER LISTENING TO YOU"?

SH: Once a man gives his answer to whatever question you're asking (or he thinks he heard, even if you never asked one), he's probably not listening to you anymore. Your cue is when he gives an answer. As far as he's concerned, his solution will fix whatever it is you're talking about, and if you're still talking after that, he's not listening anymore.

DO MEN LIKE WOMEN WHO COOK MORE THAN WOMEN WHO DON'T?

SH: That "I don't cook thing" is really big, now. If you're gorgeous and you don't cook, we can kind of overlook it. But if we're married and you're not hooking yourself up like you used to and you don't cook? You're asking too much—you're taking us for granted. Men appreciate a woman who can put together a meal. Here's good news for you women who can't cook: all of the cooking issues you have in the kitchen can be balanced out if you can really cook in the bedroom.

DO MEN SECRETLY EVALUATE WHETHER YOU'LL BE A GOOD MOTHER, HOMEMAKER, AND SO ON?

SH: Absolutely. When we're considering whether to get into a committed relationship with you, we're thinking about what our house will be like, whether you'll be a good mother, if you'll be able to handle the finances and make sound decisions. You should be evaluating us in the same fashion.

HOW DO MEN FEEL ABOUT THE WAY A WOMAN KEEPS HER HOUSE?

SH: Men cannot stand women who are not clean. When our boys come over, do you really think we want to show them a junky house? Are we really going to invite our mothers over to sit on a couch in a nasty living room? I don't think so. How the house looks is a reflection of you; people aren't going to walk in and say, "He sure keeps a dirty house"; they're going to say, "She sure keeps a dirty house." No matter how society changes or how many responsibilities men take on in the household, the bottom line is that everyone still expects the woman to turn a house into a home—a clean home. We men are no different. We like it when you put out the candles and the floral arrangements and the china and the silver, and we like to walk into a clean house. Now if we're both working and you don't have time to keep it up, and I don't want to keep it up, then we need to carve out some cash to get a housekeeper! But the house simply cannot be dirty.

ARE MEN LOOKING FOR SPECIFIC DETAILS, LIKE CREDIT, WHEN THEY'RE CONSIDERING LONG-TERM COMMITMENT?

SH: Yes. It determines how much we're going to have to work, and how much fixing we're going to have to do to provide for you. Now, it may not be a deal breaker. But it could certainly be a factor that men weigh.

WOULD A MAN FOLLOW A WOMAN WHO HAS TO MOVE BECAUSE OF HER CAREER?

SH: We'll follow you to a new job if we're secure in our manhood and confident we can still provide for you the way we want and need to. But if we have to lose everything we've worked to build to do it, and there's not evidence that we'll be able to pick up the pieces while you're working your new job, then it's going to be a tough fight.

WILL MEN GO TO COUNSELING?

SH: We're only interested in it if it's going to save our ass. If we think we're going to lose you and counseling will keep us together, then we'll go. But if it won't save our ass, we can't see any good reason why we should sit on a couch and talk to a person with a tablet, getting judged for every move we've ever made.

HOW DO MEN FEEL ABOUT SURPRISES?

SH: We like them. But please don't expect the same reaction you would have. We're not going to go to pieces and cry because you brought home a gift or planned a special trip or put together a nice, romantic surprise dinner for us. That's, well, not very manly.

DO MEN WORRY ABOUT THEIR WOMAN CHEATING?

SH: For the most part, we don't worry about it to the extent that women do, because we know your makeup is different from ours. You're more careful about the mates you choose, and you have higher standards when it comes to deciding who you will sleep with. In our minds, this drastically cuts down the likelihood of our women cheating.

ACKNOWLEDGMENTS

I would like to acknowledge the fabulous listeners of the *Steve Harvey Morning Show* who have inspired me with their questions concerning relationships.

I would like to thank Denene Millner, who had the daunting task of taking my words and my sometimes unique phrases, putting them on paper, and making them readable by people in the human race. In other words I used her as a translator and she has managed in a wonderful way to make my thoughts quite enjoyable and insightful to read.

To Shirley Strawberry, my cohost of the morning show, and to Elvira Guzman, my publicist: The two of them sat through every single writing session and every single editing session and bombarded me with questions, scenarios, and things from the female's perspective that we as men could never possibly know. These two very different viewpoints, one from a single female with no kids and the other from a woman who has a child and has been divorced, allowed me to get a wide spectrum of questions, and without them this book would not have been as thorough.

At Amistad I would like to thank Dawn Davis, who found us, Bryan Christian, who helped bring us to market, and Katherine Beitner, who helped spread the word.

To my wife, Marjorie, who has made my life so full, so complete, and, most important, so peacefully happy that it has allowed me to sit down and think beyond my current circumstance. Her cheerful spirit has made me a more cheerful person and that has allowed me to be far more sharing than I've ever been.

And to my heavenly Father who has created every blessing I have ever known in my lifetime, I give him all the glory the honor and the praise.